Lectio Divina

Revelation and Prophecy

Previous books by the author

Creating Classrooms of Peace in English Language Teaching (2022)
ISBN 9780367692148

English L2 Reading: Getting to the Bottom, 4th Edition (2021) (with
Sean Fulop)
ISBN 9780367027896

English Grammar Pedagogy: A Global Perspective (2014)
ISBN 9780415885850

The English Language Teacher in Global Civil Society (2009)
ISBN 9780415994491

Learning and Teaching English Grammar, K–12 (2004)
ISBN 9780130488343

Lectio Divina

Revelation and Prophecy

Barbara Birch

CHRISTIAN ALTERNATIVE
BOOKS

London, UK
Washington, DC, USA

CollectiveInk

First published by Christian Alternative Books, 2025
Christian Alternative Books is an imprint of Collective Ink Ltd.,
Unit 11, Shepperton House, 89 Shepperton Road, London, N1 3DF
office@collectiveinkbooks.com
www.collectiveinkbooks.com
www.christian-alternative.com

For distributor details and how to order please visit the 'Ordering' section on our website.

Text copyright: Barbara Birch 2023

ISBN: 978 1 80341 721 9
978 1 80341 740 0 (ebook)
Library of Congress Control Number: 2023950969

A CIP catalogue record for this book is available from the British Library.

Design: Lapiz Digital Services

UK: Printed and bound by CPI Group (UK) Ltd, Croydon, CR0 4YY
Printed in North America by CPI GPS partners

We operate a distinctive and ethical publishing philosophy in all areas of our business, from our global network of authors to production and worldwide distribution.

Contents

Acknowledgements

I thank my husband and family for their unconditional and unquestioning love and encouragement. You are my rock. I am grateful to beloved F(f)riends in all of my Zoom groups, Ben Lomond Quaker Center, and Friends General Conference. Special thanks to my sisters of faith who read this manuscript and commented on it. I acknowledge all the spiritual writers, living and not living, who have given me inspiration.

Chapter 1

Reading with the Indwelling

There is not in the world a kind of life more sweet
and delightful, than that of a continual conversation
with God; those only can comprehend it who
practice and experience it.

Brother Lawrence[1]

A few weeks before the pandemic, in meeting for worship,
I posed myself a question about how I could deepen my
spiritual life because my worship felt empty and pointless. My
inner guide gave me the answer, to use my natural interests
and abilities rather than trying something that was not "me."
I remembered how I read dense texts in graduate school,
stopping to summarize and take notes at each paragraph, so
that I could assimilate difficult ideas. I took this germ of an idea
and tried reading in an embodied and devotional way. When
lockdown began, I began to practice sacred reading and writing
with Thomas Kelly's essay "The Light Within," from his book
A Testament of Devotion.

Sacred reading and writing are slow and deliberate prayer
practices, starting from a sacred text and leading to deep
personal transformation. *Lectio divina* is one form of sacred
reading and prayer practiced among Christian religious orders
for hundreds of years. Traditionally, in monasteries, the
Bible was the sacred text, and its passages were transmitted
orally and memorized. Monks and nuns read passages aloud,
repeated them, and learned them to provide mental fodder for
deliberation, meditation and contemplation as they went about
their daily work. In modern formulations of lectio divina, any
kind of inspirational poetry or prose, be it religious, theistic or

non-theistic, is appropriate. The Trappist monk Thomas Merton suggested starting with modern writers who use modern language, and even writers who present non-Christian forms of spirituality.[2] Somehow, I knew that Thomas Kelly's essay would be a good way for me to start.

My intention was to approach and try to understand Brother Lawrence's "continual conversation with God" by way of Kelly's reflections on the monk and his method. "Mental habits of inward orientation must be established. An inner, secret turning to God can be made fairly steady, after weeks and months and years of practice and lapses and failures and returns. It is as simple an art as Brother Lawrence found it, but it may be long before we achieve any steadiness in the process."[3] My initial question was how did Brother Lawrence maintain a conversation with God? How could anyone maintain a constant dialogue with Spirit while at the same time carry on a normal life?

Normally, I read fast, too fast. I devour texts, rarely getting any nuances, and cannot remember what I read afterwards. In sacred reading, I forced myself to slow down and appreciate the words and meanings. To slow down, I read silently and "heard" the phrases and words in my head with intonation. I read at first for meaning, then again for a sense of the paragraph and sentence structure, and then once more for the etymology of the words. I also read aloud, listening to the sounds in the syllables and words. I read and chanted paragraphs with exaggerated intonation and hand gestures. I did not memorize paragraphs though I got to know them very well. The continual repetition of sacred words became a kind of conversation, as Brother Lawrence put it, and yet it was more about the Divine than to the Divine. The cadence was a prayer called *oratio*. I described my early lockdown experiences with sacred reading and writing in a short article in *Western Friend*.[4]

Scriptio divina is the complementary practice of writing and journaling in response to sacred texts. From the beginning, I honored certain preferences in my practice. I wanted to write by hand because I spend a lot of time keyboarding. I knew that psycholinguistic research showed that typewriting and handwriting involve different processes in the brain. Cursive writing requires carefully coordinated hand movements like drawing figures, while typing involves cruder finger movements to hit keys. Handwriting activates the brain's learning systems more than typing. Askvik et al. found that "The use of pen and paper gives the brain more 'hooks' to hang your memories on. Writing by hand creates much more activity in the sensorimotor parts of the brain. A lot of senses are activated by pressing the pen on paper, seeing the letters you write and hearing the sound you make while writing. These sense experiences create contact between different parts of the brain and open the brain up for learning. We both learn better and remember better."[5]

I got out an old fountain pen that my father made for me because I did not want to use a throwaway plastic pen, and I bought a bottle of ink at a neighborhood stationery store. I got accustomed to inky fingers. After reading a paragraph of "The Light Within," I copied it out word for word into a journal. Reading the paragraphs occupied my eyes and brain; writing them involved muscle memory and movements in my eyes, brain, arm, hands, and fingers. The extra mind/body processing helped me understand Kelly's words better, and through them, Brother Lawrence's practice of the Presence. I remembered the sentences while I walked around the neighborhood and later at home, I wrote the reconstructed sentences in my journal.

When I processed meanings in my own words, I made mind/heart associations recollected from the past. This is *meditatio*. Sometimes the words trailed off after a kind of wakeful opening, which I wrote about afterwards. This is what ancient monks and nuns called *contemplatio*. *Meditatio* and *contemplatio* seem intimidating, and yet, my insights were not earthshattering even though they were helpful to me.

Figure 1 shows how I worked with Kelly's mid-twentieth-century masculine language to add concepts of my own. *Shekinah* was a new word for me; the word refers to a symbol of divine feminine presence on earth that Kelly associates with the pronoun "it." Kelly's thoughts on mental habits of prayer got through to me. On Sundays, while centering in worship, my inner experience continued to shift from the back of my brain lower to my throat and then to my heart.

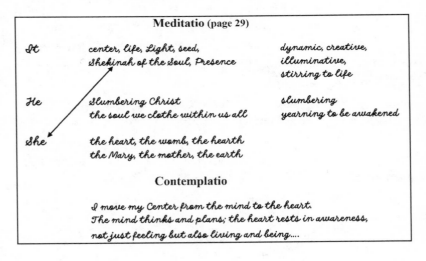

One of the fruits of lectio divina is continual insight. Days later, *contemplatio* of Kelly's essay, shown in Figure 2, opened some deeply ambivalent and thought-provoking feelings. Benedictine Sister Joan Chittister described her ongoing experience of private reflection after lectio divina like this: "The monastic cell gives me the privacy I need to continue what lectio has prompted in me: the need to recognize, to reshape what is going on within my soul right now. To discover what it is that is agitating me, preoccupying me, distracting me, holding me back from becoming the rest of who I am meant to be. The questions that seep up through lectio are legion..."[6]

Meditatio (page 42)

in the garden, day and night
winter and summer, sunshine and shadow
heat and cold, ecstasy and serenity
Spirit is here, we are with Spirit
held in tenderness, children in paradise...

Contemplatio

serenity, unshakeableness, firmness of life-orientation—
what does this mean in the face of clear signs of going the wrong way?
I'm not an established woman, very far from it.
Loss, humiliation, disappointment
are the results of vulnerability this time. Accept....

A year later I agreed to facilitate an online workshop on lectio divina based on Kelly's essay.[7] When the time came to prepare the materials, I realized that my leading to study and practice sacred reading and writing had a longer history and a larger context than I had originally thought. Decades ago, when I was a graduate student, I read *The Way of a Pilgrim*, where the pilgrim walked across Eastern Europe embedding the mantra "Lord Jesus Christ, Son of God, have mercy on me, a sinner" into his heart and soul. I reread the book and discovered that the pilgrim's method had more to it than I remembered. He carried a Bible and a copy of the *Philokalia*, a sacred text about prayer and contemplation among the Eastern Orthodox monasteries with him, repeatedly read them, and pondered them for months on end while he walked.

I recalled that in 2005 I taught a general education course called Language and Culture at my university. The textbook was Nicholas Ostler's *Empires of the Word* (HarperCollins 2003), a challenging history of the world written from the perspective of the spread of languages and their writing systems. Reading that book was where I first found myself fascinated by the intersection of linguistic modalities, religious practices, and rituals of orality and literacy in sacred languages and texts within the history of world religions. Although we now think of scripture as written texts, in fact, the ancients first performed scripture as liturgy.

For a more modern point of view and chronology, I listened to and later read Karen Armstrong's excellent book *The Lost Art of Scripture: Rescuing the Sacred Texts* (Knopf 2019). I need to mention how different my experience was in listening to and reading this book. Listening and reading employ very similar psycholinguistic knowledge of words, grammar, and meanings but the two experiences are different. I listened to Armstrong's book while walking outside so it became an active meditation. Armstrong read the text herself so I could hear emotions in her voice and accent, and developed empathy for her as an engagingly real woman. Her delivery was lively and kept my interest because it had a social element. Listening is slower and forces me to hear and process every word.

I had similar experiences with other books. For instance, listening to Cole Arthur Riley read her book *This Here Flesh: Spirituality, Liberation, and the Stories That Make Us* (Convergent 2022). was an entirely different experience from reading her book. Both versions are fabulous, and yet I much preferred listening to her exquisite voice because of the depth of empathy her perspective as a Black woman gave me. Similarly, I was reduced to tears listening to *Sacred Earth, Sacred Soul: Celtic Wisdom for Reawakening to What Our Souls Know and Healing the World* written by John Philip Newell, and superbly performed by Angus King (HarperCollins 2021). The written text was beautiful, and yet without the same gut-wrenching effect.

How differently we process and understand stories in text (visually) from how we process speech through hearing! The sensual experience of different fonts, page layouts, punctuation, and appearance in print alters the more immediate effect of the sound of accent, pause, pitch, and intonation in speech. When I combined different modalities, *lectio* and *meditatio* would occasionally dissolve into *oratio* and *contemplatio*. I also read other books to prepare for the workshop and want to highlight one: Quaker translator Sarah Ruden's *The Face of Water: A Translator on Beauty and Meaning in the Bible* (Pantheon Books, 2017). Ruden gave me a close look at the meanings and poetry of the Hebrew Bible, the Greek New Testament books, and the various translations of the sacred texts into English.

Although lectio divina came down to us from Catholicism, it is consistent with Quaker practice too. It is reading with the Indwelling, as a spiritual practice leading to transformative revelation, prophetic ministry, and embodied worship. It is body prayer, that is, it manifests in the body along with or instead of words. Believers incorporate the body into prayer and prayer into the body in many faith communities: the sign of the cross and genuflection (Roman Catholicism), touching or kissing a mezuzah in Judaism, and prostrations (*sajadat* in Islam, *panipāta* in Buddhism). In Quakerism, there is room for body prayer. Earlham theologian Grace Ji-Sun Kim wrote, "We need to work towards some form of reconciliation between the body and the mind; we need to treat the body as just as important as the mind. We can try that by practicing body prayer ... we pray to put ourselves right into God's hands, free at God's disposition, vulnerable, listening to the Divine's voice which speaks to our most honest self.... Body prayer tries to eliminate the dualistic frame of mind and reminds us that the body is good. Body prayer is our entire being praying, which is what God requires of us."[8]

When holy words and sacred concepts sink from the eyes and narrative brain to the inarticulate heart and stomach, they make fertile ground in the soul for the voice of the Divine.

Endnotes

1   Brother Lawrence of the Resurrection, OCD (c. 1614–1691) was a lay brother in a Carmelite monastery in Paris. His spiritual wisdom was compiled after his death and published as the classic Christian text, *The Practice of the Presence of God.* Grand Rapids: MI: Spire 1967, p 44.

2   Merton, Thomas, *Lectio Divina. Cistercian Studies Quarterly* 50.1 2015, 5–37.

3   Kelly, Thomas, *A Testament of Devotion*, Harper Collins Publishing, 1941, p. 38–39.

4   Birch, Barbara, "Embodying the Words of Thomas Kelly," *Western Friend*, November 2021. https://westernfriend.org/issue/95.

5   Askvik, E., van der Weel, F. R., & van der Weel, A., "The Importance of Cursive Handwriting Over Typewriting for Learning in the Classroom: A High-Density EEG Study of 12-Year-Old Children and Young Adults." Retrieved 11/1/2023 from https://www.frontiersin.org/articles/10.3389/fpsyg.2020.01810/full.

6   Chittister, Joan, *The Monastic Heart: 50 Simple Practices for a Contemplative and Fulfilling Life*, Convergent Books, 2021, p. 68.

7   Birch, Barbara, "Embodying the Light Within," workshop offered February–March 2023 at Ben Lomond Quaker Center. Around 20 Friends gathered on Zoom once a week in the evening for 5 weeks. We read the essay "The Light Within," copied paragraphs word for word, responded to the ideas in writing and worship-sharing, and practiced Centering Prayer. I encouraged participants to practice

lectio, oratio, meditatio, and contemplatio with the passages we didn't cover in the online sessions.

8   Kim, Grace Ji-Sun, "Body Prayer for Every Day," Retrieved 10/10/2023 from https://www.spiritualityhealth.com/articles/2021/02/08/body-prayer-for-every-day.

Chapter 2

Preparing for Worship

> We come to the monastery not only to praise God, or
> to obey God, but also and above all to know God in
> that knowledge which flows from love and leads to
> more love. Knowledge and love must go together.
> They must complete and assist one another, and
> bring us deep into the mystery of Christ.
>
> **Thomas Merton**

Brother Thomas Merton links knowledge and Love to offer
a purpose for lectio divina: readers, with deep, slow, and
meditative preparation, come into the knowledge and love of
Spirit before entering the Meetinghouse. People often read for
the gist of the message, scanning for specific information, or
skimming over difficult or descriptive parts. Merton emphasizes
that sacred reading is a form of prayer itself.

> Avoid the kind of reading in which nothing registers, in
> which words pass before you and you turn pages, and in
> which after it is all over, you do not remember what you
> have read. Reading should be fruitful and productive. It
> should stimulate thought and lead to deeper prayer. It
> should be not merely an occasion of prayer (I have the
> book in my hand, and occasionally turn aside to pray—
> but not moved by anything I read)—it should stimulate
> and inspire prayer as an efficient cause.[1]

Usually, people read as quickly as possible, to tick off a book
from a list or to find out how the book ends. Lectio divina is
the opposite. Benedictine Sister Joan Chittister offers another

purpose for lectio divina: to put readers into an uncomfortable heart space that prods them to start a conversation with Spirit about life, and right-living, in wisdom and Love. She wrote,

> Sacred reading is what stops us from dashing through spiritual ideas without stopping to consider exactly what they mean to us today. Or actually meant to anybody— even in the times when they were first read. In fact, sacred reading is not an exercise in reading the greatest number of holy books we can get our hands on. On the contrary, sacred reading is about prodding thought, not finishing pages. It is meant to begin a long and deliberate conversation with God about what it means to be alive, to be holy, to be "in the Spirit," to be a disciple—here and now.[2]

There is a possible third purpose. Lectio divina fuses reading to contemplative prayer in a practice that moves us toward our better selves with a sense of the Indwelling that renews us. It relies on metaphor, imagination, and play. My hypothesis is that lectio divina allows readers to bridge the divide between the two hemispheres of the brain. The left side is analytical, rational, judgmental, critical, and logical and the right side is emotional, intuitive, accepting, and open to seeing interconnections and unions.

And yet, there is a paradox in that, like with all spiritual practices, lectio divina should not be performed with specific aims in mind. Benedictine priest Luke Dysinger reminds the reader, "We must be willing to sacrifice our 'goal-oriented' approach if we are to practice lectio divina, because lectio divina has no other goal than spending time with God through the medium of his word.... Lectio divina teaches us to savor and delight in all the different flavors of God's presence, whether they be active or receptive modes of experiencing him."[3] If we hold specific ideas of what we want to achieve, we may inadvertently close our hearts, minds, and souls to learning that comes in unexpected ways.

And yet, despite this paradox, I come back to this. Quakers have no division between priesthood and laity; we are all meant to minister to each other and to receive ministry during Meeting for Worship. Maybe some seekers, like me, want to perceive more fullness in a silence that seems empty, dry and dormant. Maybe we want to grow our connection to the Gathering Spirit by learning about the worship encounters of spiritual ancestors or contemporaries. Some of us may want to nurture our own sacred wisdom to offer to our faith community as ministry. Together we may yearn to hear the kind of vocal ministry that leads to group mysticism of the disciplined soul and the disciplined group.[4] In such Gathered Meetings, vocal ministry doesn't break the silence but continues it with messages that recall the human-divine union, or humble prayers that take Friends deeper into worship. Still, these reasons must be subordinate to the blessing and grace of spending time with sources and streams of wisdom and Love from sacred words.

Many liberal Friends today put the sanctity of silence over the blessings of ministry, but the opposite was the original intention. Christine Simmons, in a post about vocal ministry on social media, summarized the situation in liberal Quakerism very succinctly, writing, "There was much more ministry amongst early Quakers. We should remember that the silence is not an end in itself, but a liturgical tool facilitating ministry."[5] Rufus Jones wrote,

Hardly less important and significant for the spiritual life of a meeting is its constructive and creative ministry. There are perhaps some seasoned Friends who find their souls sufficiently fed in the silence, who do not need, or at least think they do not need, the ministry of spoken words. But most persons who compose a congregation are carrying burdens, often too heavy to be borne, and there are always some who are 'oppressed by the heavy and weary weight of all this unintelligible world': and who need a lift. They look for inspiration and guidance. They want to have the significance of life and the grounds of immortality brought to light.[6]

In contrast, Isaac Penington described the holistic way that early Friends worshipped.

> And this is the manner of their worship. They are to wait upon the Lord, to meet in the silence of flesh, and to watch for the stirrings of his life, and the breakings forth of his power amongst them. And in the breakings forth of that power they may pray, speak, exhort, rebuke, sing, or mourn, &c. according as the Spirit teaches, requires, and gives utterance. But if the Spirit do not require to speak, and give to utter, then everyone is to sit still in his place (in his heavenly place I mean), feeling his own measure, feeding thereupon, receiving therefrom, into his spirit, what the Lord giveth.[7]

Many Quaker tracts, sermons, and blogs advise Friends about the quality and quantity of vocal ministry. Ministry should arise from the heart, not from the intellect. It should be short and succinct. It should not be prepared ahead of time during the week. It should not be read out. Some Friends lament shallow or political vocal ministry, too many meetings with unrelieved silence, or unfiltered ministry that might discourage newcomers or visitors. There is, in fact, at least one flowchart floating around Meetings that is designed to help Friends decide if what rises for them in worship should be shared as vocal ministry or not. It can seem intimidating. Friends often feel that they don't have anything to offer in vocal ministry, or that someone else is better at it. We rely on others to preach what we are too afraid to say. These are all important and useful points to make, and yet, ministry and prophecy are always difficult, even for the most well known.

A passage in 4 Exodus 10–16[8] is a story about Moses and his brother Aaron. Moses may have had a speech impediment making him a slow or tongue-tied speaker, or maybe he was overly self-conscious and fearful. In either case, Moses was reluctant to prophesize, but the Divine put the Word in his mouth.

> Moses said to the Lord, "Pardon your servant, Lord. I have never been eloquent, neither in the past nor since you have spoken to your servant. I am slow of speech and tongue."
>
> The Lord said to him, "Who gave human beings their mouths? Who makes them deaf or mute? Who gives them sight or makes them blind? Is it not I, the Lord? Now go; I will help you speak and will teach you what to say."
>
> But Moses said, "Pardon your servant, Lord. Please send someone else."
>
> Then the Lord's anger burned against Moses and he said, "What about your brother, Aaron the Levite? I know he can speak well. He is already on his way to meet you, and he will be glad to see you.
>
> "You shall speak to him and put words in his mouth; I will help both of you speak and will teach you what to do.
>
> "He will speak to the people for you, and it will be as if he were your mouth and as if you were God to him."

Here are some quotes which indicate that vocal ministry is a concern in many Meetings:

1972: There are some persons who attend a Friends' meeting for worship with the hope that there will be no vocal ministry at all. They prefer the silence and resent messages of vocal ministry as intrusions.... But the actual truth of the matter is that meetings that have turned completely silent almost invariably wither away. Something is missing in the corporate relationship ... the practical experience of the Society of Friends, historically, knows the fate of a meeting that is habitually mute.[9]

2022: One way I like to capture the communal and public nature of vocal ministry, is by thinking of meeting for worship as a shared meal, with vocal ministry as the various dishes we prepare and offer for the table ... if the vast majority of people don't feel confident enough to bring a dish, or if the dishes that are brought are always inedible, then we need to start offering cookery classes.... Our meetings are not private, silent retreats. They are spaces for the spirit to move and do surprising things.[10]

2022: Every book of Quaker faith and practice has either a query or an advice urging Friends to come to meeting "with hearts and minds prepared." We each do this preparation differently, but two things seem to be essential. First, we need to do what is necessary to nurture our spirits during the week, through daily, or at least steady, spiritual practice.... Second, we each need to have worked through the top layer of issues on our minds and hearts in our own space and time, in our own spiritual practice, so that we have within us a spaciousness in which the Divine may have room to be present and, perhaps, to speak through us.[11]

2023: Social Media post: My experience with being a part of several meetings and visiting numerous is that many meetings have perhaps one or two Friends gifted in ministry; one or two not especially gifted who appear to like the sound of their own voices rather too much (sorry but there it is); one or two who don't really understand what ministry is and speak from their personal ethical/political/social views/philosophies; and the vast majority of Friends who never or hardly ever minister, some of whom are quenching the Spirit because they have decided of their own volition that vocal ministry is never their part, or because they feel intimidated by those more articulate. I detect little if any shared sense of responsibility for vocal ministry.[12]

These statements show a potential for lectio divina to help Spirit put sacred words in our mouths and teach us what to say in ministry. Like Moses, Friends can be the prophetic voice of the Divine.

Endnotes

1   Merton, Thomas, "Lectio Divina," *Cistercian Studies Quarterly* 50.1 (2015), pp. 5–37

2   Chittister, Joan, *The Monastic Heart: 50 Simple Practices for a Contemplative and Fulfilling Life*, Convergent Books, 2021. p 57.

3   Dysinger, Luke, "Accepting the Embrace of God: The Ancient Art of Lectio Divina,"Retrieved 9/20/2022 from chrome-extension://efaidnbmnnnibpcajpcglclefindmkaj/ https://www.oblatespring.com/Resources/LectioDivina.pdf

4   Kelly, Thomas, "The Gathered Meeting," https:// tractassociation.org/digital-material/meeting-for-worship/ the-gathered-meeting/

5   Simmons, Christine, personal communication 10/2/2023 used with permission.

6   Jones, Rufus, "The Vital Cell," Retrieved 8/8/2020 from https://quaker.org/legacy/pamphlets/wpl1941a.html

7   Penington, Isaac, "A Brief Account Concerning Silent Meetings." https://quaker.org/legacy/pamphlets/wpl1941a.html, Philadelphia, 1868. Public Domain.

8   All citations from the Bible are from the New International Version (NIV) and Retrieved from https://www.biblegateway.com/. Occasionally, I modify a few words in Spirit.

9   Steere, Douglas, "On Speaking Out of the Silence: Vocal Ministry in the Unprogrammed Meeting for Worship," PHP 182, 1972, pp. 7–8.

10 Russ, Mark, "Exploring Vocal Ministry," https://www.woodbrooke.org.uk/exploring-vocal-ministry/ July 7, 2022

11 Sammond, Christopher, "Utterly Naked Before God," June 1, 2022, https://www.friendsjournal.org/utterly-naked-before-god/

12 Barnett, Ian, personal communication 10/2/2023, used with permission.

Chapter 3

Grounding on the Earth

The first Bible is the Bible of nature. It was written at least 13.8 billion years ago, at the moment that we call the Big Bang, long before the Bible of words. Ever since God created the world, God's everlasting power and divinity—however invisible—are there for the mind to see in the things that God has made.

Richard Rohr

Richard Rohr[1] pointed out that humans and our earth home itself benefit from imagining the earth as scripture, as a Spirit-inspired work of art full of symbols and wisdom. Whether we agree on a literal creator god or not, "scriptural earth" forces us to reimagine the idea of the "Word" and our understanding of the beginning of the Gospel of John. "In the beginning was the Word, and the Word was with God, and the Word was God. The same was in the beginning with God. All things were made by him; and without him was not anything made that was made." The image of the earth as holy ground makes sense of the fact that many individuals find the most meaning, comfort, and enlightenment when they are in nature. This is the allure and mystery of the labyrinth, with its humble entrance, its prayerful walk into the center and then the return to the world after experiencing a renewal of Spirit.

The earth as Word also explains the apparently absurd notion that lectio divina may have started before reading and writing were invented. A cave by the Volp River in France has images dated to 13,000 BCE. What is interesting about this cave is that walking and crawling through it is described as "reading scripture," a scripture of the sacred Word, a "book" of sacred images and sites depicting events or beings. The cave is a way of entering into the womb of *being*.

> The drawings are often tucked between pillars or otherwise placed in a position that allows them to be viewed only from certain angles and only by a handful of people at a time, indicating that the cave—not just the images projected upon it, but the cave itself—was intended to be part of the spiritual experience. The cave becomes a mythogram; it is meant to be read, the way one reads scripture.[2]

Thousands of years later, Chittister described sacred reading itself as a cave: "Lectio… is a journey into the cave of the heart."[3]

The story of lectio divina started many millennia ago, when sacred words and beliefs were inside humans, in their memories, in their bodies, in their conversations, in their land, and in their rituals. People learned sacred words and stories by heart because there was no alternative and because they felt that the heart was the seat of memory and history. Each person understood the sacred at the gut level and lived in, with, and through the holy in their daily lives on sacred earth, with no division between the religious world and the secular world.

Many modern Western people think of faith as just one aspect of personal identity within a culture, a characteristic separable from other identifiers like ethnicity or race. To many of us, religion is a choice; people can convert from one religion to another. Everyone can accept, qualify, or reject a belief or a system of beliefs. If everyone distinguishes religion from all else, then by default, everything else is secular. Secularization has had a deep effect on our thinking and being. In contrast, the ancients did not distinguish faith from any other cultural content. In prehistory, collective human existence took place within an organic envelope of faith, history, tradition, cultural concepts, and social structures. It is hard to imagine such a time.

Social historians do not know much about the spiritual life of those who lived in early nonliterate cultures, though, to be sure, they had play, language, imagination, ritual, and storytelling, and like us, they used these to express ideas they yearned to understand.

Author Jack Miles tried to find the underlying cause of religion. Did it start in a need for explanations or in imagination and play?[4] He wrote,

> I confess that I experience a certain relief in thinking of play rather than explanation as quite possibly the evolutionary taproot of religion.... Isaac Newton—still, I think, the greatest scientist of all time—wrote famously and rather poignantly: 'I do not know what I may appear to the world; but to myself I seem to have been only a boy playing on the seashore, and diverting myself in now and then finding a smoother pebble or a prettier shell than ordinary, while the great ocean of truth lay all undiscovered before me.'[5]

Miles responded to Newton, whom he called "science personified," with a fictional retort from a boy who personified religion: "This has been fun, but it's getting dark, the tide is coming in, supper may be almost ready, and I'm going home. The ocean will still be there tomorrow. If you come along, I promise to tell you a story on the way."[6] This tongue-in-cheek answer reveals that faith offers humanity values that rationality cannot: comfort, nourishment, belonging, play, ritual, imagination, and stories.

One of the earliest precursors of faith to develop is language. Hugh Brody described it like this:

When human beings began to use language, their brain structure made an evolutionary leap of huge importance. The physiological difference between those who spoke and those who did not may have been small, a tiny fraction of the entire brain. But once it was there, a divide opened between humans and all other animals, a divide that had immense and ever-expanding consequences. Language allowed human evolution to take a very different and much more elaborate path. In the absence of language, inheritance is limited to the gene pool. Parents pass on to their offspring a bundle of genes and very little else. But with language, they can pass on vast bodies of knowledge, moral codes, forms of social arrangement. And with language, it is possible to think. With thought, it is possible for each generation to transform knowledge and ideas, which are then passed on to the generation that follows. Once it had language, the human species spread throughout the world, from environment to environment, each group with its own ways of occupying territory, knowing about their land and ordering their lives in a particular region. In this way, humans came to live in cultures—that is, in many kinds of articulate and organized societies.[7]

Cultural and linguistic behaviors like play, imagination, language, metaphor, ritual, dreaming, storytelling and learning come together in creating myths and practices of faith, and yet little is known about these embodied faiths before writing emerged in the Middle East sometime between 4000 BCE and 3001 BCE. Just because they were oral, there is no reason to think that ancient societies and cultures were somehow primitive or simple. There were elaborate burial rituals, performances, art, music, and spoken literature. Karen Armstrong suggests that the ancients revered, instead of a human-like God figure, a mysterious sense of fundamental energy, *being*, animating the world and gathering everything in the world together as one. Armstrong put it like this:

> *Being* is transcendent. You could not see, touch, or hear it but could only watch it at work in the people, objects, and natural forces around you. From the documents of later Neolithic and pastoral communities, we know that *being* rather than *a being* was revered as the ultimate sacred power. It was impossible to define or describe, because *being* is all encompassing and our minds are only equipped to deal with particular beings, which can merely participate in it in a restricted manner. But certain objects (a stone, the moon, the sky, the sun) became eloquent symbols of the power of *being*, which sustained and shone through them with particular clarity.... *Being* bound all things together; humans, animals, plants, insects, stars and birds all shared the divine life that sustained the entire cosmos.... Everything was a manifestation of this all-pervading "Spirit" (Sanskrit *manja*).[8]

Modern archeologists and historians still find traces of permanent carvings, scratches, handprints, and images of humans and animals dating back hundreds of thousands of years, from even before our primate ancestors were Homo sapiens. These ancestors believed that a mysterious transcendent (out there) and incarnate (in here) agency supported the cosmos. The earth, humans and other animals, plants, objects, and natural phenomena all had a sacred essence, soul, or spirit, and a sense of (hyper-)individuality as we know it today probably did not exist.

Humans in their natural state, that is, without knowledge of reading and writing, probably had more perceptual diversity; they could perceive, access, remember and imagine in ways we cannot. They valued sacred wisdom like magic, miracles, trance, "flow," dreams, visions, and imagination. Their world was not based on numbers and quantification, logic and syllogism, data and information, and theories and categories. Tyson Yunkaporta described different ways of thinking in Indigenous nonliterate cultures: kinship/relationships (connection and integration), stories/narratives (history and memorization), dreaming/metaphor (wisdom and knowledge), ancestor/"flow" state (learning and concentration), and patterns/trends (prediction and problem-solving).[9]

For our ancient ancestors, language was not something contained in the mind; it was in the world, as spoken interactions among neighbors. Our ancestors were unlikely to have the capacity that linguists call "language awareness," that is, awareness of language as an object of study. The idea that people can look at language as a thing and analyze it develops through schooling and literacy as learners encounter words outside themselves in books. The ancients would have been unlikely to have the idea of a "word" separated from the flow of speech or the objects they referred to in the world, except for proper names. Proper names were sacred and powerful.

Once language and culture developed, modern human consciousness emerged, and it sparked the invention of writing materials and scripts, and then its own inventions transformed consciousness itself. (We can see the same processes going on with the invention of the personal computer and the iPhone.)

Some researchers believe that the invention of writing, especially the alphabets composed of vowels and consonants, started the process of bilateralization in the brain, and left-brain dominance. Before that, the hemispheres of the brain operated as balanced partners, as they are in preliterate children today. Schooling and especially the need to process script and numbers cause the brain to transform its neural networking towards more left-brained dominance. Today, researchers find that the brains of nonliterate people are different from literate people and that Chinese readers process written language differently from English readers. The tasks that the brain performs in reading different scripts cause the development of different neural pathways and different strategies.[10]

Researchers have never found a particular physical location for our sense of the Divine, a "God spot." However, neurologists have found the right hemisphere of the brain to be crucial in the creation of poetry, music, faith, and self. It has a less focused holistic orientation to the world compared to the selective, pragmatic, and analytical left hemisphere. Children, for example, are much more prone to imaginative activities, daydreaming, visualization, and fantasy. Armstrong wrote,

> Above all [the right hemisphere] sees itself as connected to the outside world, whereas the left hemisphere holds aloof from it.... [I]t sees each thing in relation to the whole and perceives the interconnectedness of reality. It is, therefore, at home with metaphor, in which disparate entities become one....[11]

Historian Reza Aslan pointed out the paradigm-shifting influence of writing on culture, technology, and spirituality: "Writing changes everything. Its development marks the dividing line between prehistory and history. The entire reason why Mesopotamia is known as the Cradle of Civilization is because sometime in the fourth millennium BCE, the Sumerians began to press blunt reed styluses into wet clay to make the distinctive wedge-shaped lines we call cuneiform, allowing human beings, for the first time in history, to record their most abstract thoughts...."[12] Language, writing, and consciousness make the ancient creation myths in the Hebrew Bible Book of Genesis intriguing. In the first myth, God is *ruach* (feminine spirit, breath or wind in Hebrew), a force which gathered nature and made it spring into *being*. *Ruach* initiated language and started the earthly time clock. The myth in 1 Genesis 1 reflects much older formulaic and ritualistic creation stories that were common in many cultures at the time.

In the beginning, when God created the universe,
the earth was formless and desolate.
The raging ocean that covered everything
was engulfed in total darkness,
and the Spirit of God [ruach] was moving over the water.
Then God initiated, "Let there be light"—and light
appeared.
God was pleased with what God saw.
Then God initiated a separation between the light from
the darkness,
and God named the light "Day" and the darkness "Night."
Evening passed and morning came—that was the first
day.

The second part of the myth, in 2 Genesis, is a narrative that may date from 500 BCE, long after the invention and spread of writing, when the editors combined various creation myths into one sacred text. Our ancestors realized that spoken language was an essential characteristic of being human (although not everyone can speak). By that time, "God" operated as a humanlike all-powerful tireless workingman even though God took a day of rest every seven days. The story describes how God called on the first human to name each living creature; naming symbolized human dominion over other animals and nature. No other creature was worthy of being a companion to Adam.

And out of the ground God formed every beast of the
field

and every bird of the air,
and God brought them to the man to see what he would
name each one.
And whatever the man called each living creature, that
was its name.
The man gave names to all the livestock, to the birds of
the air,
and to every beast of the field. But for Adam no suitable
helper was found.

Do these two myths document a fundamental change in human
consciousness? It is plausible to think that the idea of the Divine
as an animistic Spirit, *being*, or *ruach* existed for many millennia
until the new technology of writing began, and humans began
to translate spoken words to hard surfaces using visual marks.
Aslan identified the reification of the concept of God as by-
product of sacred writing.

> The act of writing about the gods, of being forced to
> describe in words what the gods are like, not only
> transformed how we envision the gods; it made conscious
> and explicit our unconscious and implicit desire to make
> the gods in our own image. The very words we choose
> to describe the gods affect how we understand their
> nature, their personality, even their physical form. For
> example, the word for "god" in Sumerian is *ilu*, which
> means something like "lofty person" and so that became
> precisely how the gods were envisioned in Sumerian
> writings: as elevated beings who had human bodies and
> wore human clothes, who expressed human emotions
> and exhibited human personalities.[13]

One of the first types of explicit language awareness that
develops in humans, and therefore in civilizations, is noticing

that different populations speak different incomprehensible languages. The myth that explains language diversity is the Tower of Babel story in 11 Genesis 1–9. The myth features a God who feels threatened by humans and their productivity when they cooperate, and he starts messing with their speech so they cannot understand each other and waste time competing and making war.

> Now the whole earth had one language and the same words.
> And as they migrated from the east, they came upon a plain
> in the land of Shinar and settled there.
> And they said to one another, "Come, let us make bricks and fire them thoroughly." And they had brick for stone and bitumen for mortar.
> Then they said, "Come, let us build ourselves a city and a tower with its top in the heavens, and let us make a name for ourselves; otherwise, we shall be scattered abroad upon the face of the whole earth."
> The Lord came down to see the city and the tower, which mortals had built.
> And the Lord said, "Look, they are one people, and they have all one language, and this is only the beginning of what they will do; nothing that they propose to do will now be impossible for them.
> "Come, let us go down and confuse their language there, so that they will not understand one another's speech."
> So the Lord scattered them abroad from there over the face of all the earth, and they left off building the city.
> Therefore it was called Babel, because there the Lord confused (balal) the language of all the earth, and from there the Lord scattered them abroad over the face of all the earth.

The words humans use to conceptualize the Divine and how humans relate to the Divine are important. Is the Divine up in the sky as a supreme judge or a transcendent man-god? Can the Divine mess with humans and cause bad things to happen? Is the Divine the ground of *being* that gathers us together as Friends? Is the Divine inside our bodies and souls as a spirit of Love? Is there any separation between the human and the Divine? These questions are beyond any dichotomy between theistic and humanistic beliefs. Quaker humanist David Boulton thinks that "There is no meaningful conflict between the human-centred and the God-centred. If God is no more (but, gloriously, no less) than a projection of our highest and deepest values, and if these must be human values (because no other form of life has created and articulated them), God-centredness just becomes one way, a religious way, of talking about being human."

Endnotes

1   Rohr, Richard, *The First Bible*. Retrieved 8/15/2022 from https://cac.org/daily-meditations/the-first-bible-2016-02-28/ Sunday, February 28, 2016.

2   Aslan, Reza, *God: A Human History*, Random House 2017, p. 14.

3   Chittister, Joan, *The Monastic Heart: 50 Simple Practices for a Contemplative and Fulfilling Life*, Convergent Books, 2021. p. 57

4   Miles, Jack, *Religion as We Know it: An Origin Story*, W.W. Norton & Company, 2019, p. 139 ebook.

5   Newton, Isaac, quoted in Sir David Brewster, *The Life of Sir Isaac Newton*, J. and J. Harper, 1831 pp. 300–301 cited in Miles, p. 139 ebook.

6   Miles, Jack, *Religion as We Know it: An Origin Story*, W.W. Norton & Company, 2019, p. 139 ebook.

7   Brody, Hugh, *The Other Side of Eden, Hunters, Farmers, and the Shaping of the World*, Farrar, Straus, and Giroux, 2000, p. 279.

8   Armstrong, Karen, *The Lost Art of Scripture: Rescuing the Sacred Texts*, Knopf 2019, p. 9.

9   Yunkaporta, Tyson, *Sand Talk: How Indigenous Thinking Can Save the World*, Harper One, an imprint of HarperCollins Publications, 2020.

10   Birch, Barbara and Sean Fulop, *English L2 Reading: Getting to the Bottom*, 4th edition, Routledge 2020.

11   Armstrong, Karen, *The Lost Art of Scripture: Rescuing the Sacred Texts*, Knopf 2019, p. 5.

12   Aslan, Reza, *God: A Human History*, Random House, 2017, ebook p. 1.

13   Aslan, Reza, *God: A Human History*, Random House, 2017, ebook p. 73.

14   Boulton, David, *The Faith of a Quaker Humanist*, Quaker Universalist Group 1997 Retrieved 4/3/2023 from https://nontheist-quakers.org.uk/articles/the-faith-of-a-quaker-humanist/

Chapter 4

Constraining the Word in Script

Lectio, then is the practice of extracting from every
sentence, every phrase, every word of a psalm or
Gospel passage, its meaning for the reader at this
time, in this age.

Joan Chittister

For Benedictine Sister Joan Chittister, lectio divina is a way
for readers to find in the sacred text meanings that came
from personal experience at a specific time in history.[1] Lectio
divina makes the passage come alive in imagination rooted
in visualizing a particular time and place. Meanings are not
past facts and information or future conjectures and wishes;
they are constructions and reconstructions of memories, body
sensations, emotions, events, and relationships in the present.
Meanings are unique to each reader; they access recollections
and images from mental associations with words and phrases.
Lectio divina is meant to be a whole brain activity, holistic,
metaphorical, playful, and liturgical. This type of reading has
always been historically important.

The earliest mention of reading and writing in the Hebrew
Bible is in Exodus 17:14, from the time of Moses, possibly 1250
BCE. "After the victory, the Lord instructed Moses, 'Write this
down on a scroll as a permanent reminder, and read it aloud
to Joshua: I will erase the memory of Amalek from under
heaven.'" Moses had specially trained scribes and scroll-makers
to record the threat so that it would not be forgotten. Readers
understand that the pragmatic effect of the threat came from
the oral performance of the words; the statement created a
promise of a dire consequence. Threats, vows, and promises

are performatives. The words on the scroll recorded the verbal threat in an external memory and constrained it for all history. That is what writing was for at the time: recording speech.

Long before that first record, around the year 3000 BCE, Egyptians invented papyrus, a writing material perfect for ink made from carbon and oil. They used hieroglyphs to write religious literature on papyrus and wood, and later, monumental inscriptions. Hieroglyphic writing itself endured in use for a long time, and one of its daughter systems, the Phoenician alphabet, gave rise to the alphabets all around the Mediterranean Sea and beyond. The earliest Hebrew writing system recycled hieroglyphs for a script attested in various inscriptions from 2100–1500 BCE. The oral Torah (Law or Instruction) probably dates from around 1000–900 BCE or before. Hebrew scribes did not write it down until much later, around 539 BCE when the Hebrew people returned from their captivity in Babylon. That makes the timings of events in the Bible confusing because the scribes in 539 BCE recombined, rewrote or even reinvented their prehistory as history in their own terms.

Bellah provides some key dates in the chronology of biblical events, adapted here.[2]

Hebrew speaking/some writing?	1250 BCE	Moses[34] (traditional dating)
	1208 BCE	First mention of Israel in Egyptian records
	1030-930 BCE	Saul, David, Solomon as Kings
	930-722 BCE	Divided kingdoms of Judah (S) and Israel (N)
	722 BCE	Assyrian conquest of Israel
	587 BCE	Babylonian conquest of Judah
Aramaic & Hebrew diglossia	587-538 BCE	Babylonian Exile (written Torah in Hebrew)
	538 BCE	Exiles start returning to Judah
koiné Greek, Aramaic, & Hebrew triglossia	333 BCE	Alexander conquers Persian Empire (Judah)
	65 BCE	Roman conquest of Palestine

In prehistorical times, the Torah did not yet exist in script, although the concept of sacred writing already existed. God's name was so holy and powerful that humans could not speak it, and they had to find circumlocutions like the LORD, YHWH, and later Adonai in speech and later in writing. The word "scripture" is related to script but it refers specifically to sacred, holy, or supernatural uses of writing. In Exodus, Hebrew writing was associated with God; it was highly symbolic and powerful. When people inscribed sacred words on animal skins, papyrus, or parchment scrolls, or clay or metal tablets and stones, words began to exist outside the human body for the first time. Crucially for the history of lectio divina, sacred words reified sacred concepts and placed them in external storage for all history.

Furthermore, writing legitimized and standardized oral texts. Scriptures became property, and objects that could be given away, stolen, hidden, destroyed, censored, or even broken. God inscribed the ten commandments on stone tablets and gave them to Moses, who probably did not know how to write. Moses broke the tablets in a fit of rage and God had to rewrite them. Written symbols were powerful. God commanded the high priest Aaron, the brother of Moses, to wear two stones engraved with the names of the sons of Israel on his shoulders and a gold plate engraved with the words *Holy to the Lord* as a seal on his forehead. With these symbols, God marked Aaron as his spokesman and prophet, and made him responsible for the sacred gifts the Israelites consecrated in their worship.

Around 590 BCE, after some military defeats, the Judean leadership and twenty percent of the population were forcibly relocated from Judah to Babylon in an act of ethnic cleansing. Babylonians destroyed the city of Jerusalem and when they burned the temple to the ground in 586 BCE, they destroyed Israel's sacred texts, and yet priestly scribes preserved the Torah in their hearts. They transmitted the traditions and collective wisdom from mouths to ears in rhythmic and figurative language designed to be easily remembered, and then set them down in writing just as they were remembered. In their retelling, scribes made little distinction between history, faith, and Law because the religious and the secular world were not distinct. The passages were edited and reassembled as a patchwork of different sources, which accounts for some of the inconsistencies and redundancies in the Hebrew Bible as we know it today. Meanwhile, the displaced Judeans assimilated to Babylonia and spoke Aramaic instead of Hebrew.

Once scroll-makers filled all the papyrus or animal skin surfaces with writing, they sewed them into long strips and wound the strips on two dowel-like wooden pieces. In the right environment, scrolls lasted for centuries. Unlike their depiction in films, scrolls were unwieldly and difficult to manipulate, although they were better than rocks and clay tablets. Each scroll contained a separate piece of literature. The Bible did not exist as a sequence of related books, and no spaces or numbers separated chapters and verses. The meaning of the words was still in the oral performance of the words, not the writings, which were merely "notes" for the performer.

By the time King Cyrus of Persia conquered Babylonia and allowed the Judeans to return home in 538 BCE, the Torah scrolls were complete. They were in Hebrew so Aramaic readers needed to learn Hebrew to read them. The culture was diglossic—that is, people habitually used Aramaic for daily use and Hebrew for sacred use. The scribes preserved their wisdom heritage from before the captivity and, henceforth, Judeans would be called "people of the book." The scrolls helped them recover and reformulate their lost and fractured culture, history, rituals, and faith after their forced resettlement and return. In this case, at least, rote memory and written scrolls proved to be more powerful than genocide.

One such scribe and prophet was Ezra (480 BCE–440 BCE), a man who "devoted himself to the study and observance of the Law of the Lord, and to teaching its decrees and laws in Israel" (7 Ezra 10). Karen Armstrong wrote that the story of the

Torah was mysterious, "writing under divine inspiration, Ezra had restored them spending forty days dictating ninety-four of these books to scribes. Yet he withheld seventy important texts that could be imparted at some future time only to the wisest Israelites. These texts were never disclosed. This was a myth that expressed an important truth: in scripture, there is always something left unsaid."[3]

In 8 Nehemiah 2–3, Nehemiah, the governor (473 BCE–403 BCE), tells how Ezra helped the Hebrew people recover their wisdom and culture:

> So on the first day of the seventh month Ezra the priest brought the Law before the assembly, which was made up of men and women and all who were able to understand. He read it aloud from daybreak till noon as he faced the square before the Water Gate in the presence of the men, women and others who could understand. And all the people listened attentively to the Book of the Law.

I imagine Ezra performing from a high stage using the scrolls as cues to evoke the Hebrew words that he already knew by heart. While Ezra performed, priests and teachers went among the gathered people, translating to Aramaic, commenting, answering questions, and clarifying meanings, so that everyone could inscribe the essence of the text on their hearts.

The story about Ezra may contain the earliest documented example of Jewish *exegesis*. Exegesis is the Greek name for the painstaking critical study, interpretation and elaboration of the scripture, called *midrash* in Hebrew. Midrash is "a Jewish mode of interpretation that not only engages the words of the text, behind the text, and beyond the text, but also focuses on each letter, and the words left unsaid by each line."[4] Through the centuries, the original Hebrew words have multiplied into numerous other commentaries and interpretations that update the meanings. Midrash required students to develop a deeply embodied understanding of the holy words. Exegesis is the precursor to lectio divina. In later centuries, they would split off from each other because their functions and purposes differ. Both types of reading start with deep study, but lectio divina makes readers into seekers and pray-ers. Armstrong wrote, "[U]nlike exegesis, which determined the meaning of ancient text, [lectio divina] was designed to cultivate an attitude of prayer and an apprehension of the divine presence."[5]

After the long days of grueling midrash together, 8 Nehemiah 10–12 records how Nehemiah ordered the people to gather, feast and share their plenty with others, even strangers, because their cultural identity, sacred knowledge, and homeland were restored.

> Nehemiah said, "Go and enjoy choice food and sweet
>   drinks,
> and send some to those who have nothing prepared.
> This day is holy to our Lord.
> Do not grieve, for the joy of the Lord is your strength."
> The Levites calmed all the people, saying,
> "Be still, for this is a holy day. Do not grieve."
> Then all the people went away to eat and drink,
> to send portions of food and to celebrate with great joy,
> because they now understood the words that had been
>   made known to them.

There was, indeed, a lot to celebrate. Everyone was hungry for relationship with the past, with others in the present, and with a new future together, and the sacred texts would feed them now and forever. The scrolls not only preserved the Torah; they also preserved Hebrew as a sacred language so that, over two thousand years later, Jews would speak it in synagogues around the world and in the streets of Jerusalem. The Torah preserved rituals and liturgies still used to this day. Rabbis and scholars are still very intentional about feeding men, women, and children by reciting, commenting, and clarifying to make the traditional words relevant to contemporary times.

Endnotes

1 Chittister, Joan, *The Monastic Heart: 50 Simple Practices for a Contemplative and Fulfilling Life*, Convergent Books, 2021. p 57.

2 Bellah, Robert, *Religion in Human Evolution: From the Paleolithic to the Axial Age*, Harvard University Press. 2017, p. 285.

3 Armstrong, Karen, *The Lost Art of Scripture: Rescuing the Sacred Texts*, Knopf 2019, p.109.

4 Lovelace, Vanessa, "Womanist Midrash: A Reintroduction to the Women of the Torah and the Throne," *Horizons in Biblical Theology*, by Wilda C. Gafney. 2018. 40 (2), pp. 212–215.

5 Armstrong, Karen, *The Lost Art of Scripture: Rescuing the Sacred Texts*, Knopf 2019, p. 497.

Chapter 5

Eating the Scroll

> Let us ruminate, and, as it were, chew the cud, that we may have the sweet juice, spiritual effect, marrow, honey, kernel, taste, comfort and consolation of them.
>
> **Thomas Cranmer**

Thomas Cranmer (1489–1556), Archbishop of Canterbury, did not originate the visceral metaphor of chewing, ruminating, and gnawing on sacred passages to extract their sweet juice, kernel and marrow.[1] The metaphor goes back at least two thousand years to the time of Ezekial, another Hebrew prophet who lived during the captivity in Babylon. Ezekial heard the Divine telling him to ingest and digest the message of Love and Truth (sweet as honey) to make holy wisdom an integral part of his mind and body. Only by chewing and swallowing could he understand and hold the sacred Wisdom and Truth in his soul, and so preach to others with integrity. In 3 Ezekiel 1–5, Ezekial had to "eat" the scroll.

> And he said to me, "Son of man, eat what is before you,
>   eat this scroll;
> then go and speak to the people of Israel."
> So I opened my mouth, and he gave me the scroll to eat.
> Then he said to me, "Son of man, eat this scroll I am
>   giving you
> and fill your stomach with it."
> So I ate it, and it tasted as sweet as honey in my mouth.
> He then said to me: "Son of man, go now to the people
>   of Israel

and speak my words to them.
You are not being sent to a people of obscure speech and
strange language,
but to the people of Israel—"

Eating the scroll required more than memorization of a spoken
sequence of Hebrew words; it meant making the words and
wisdom part of their body and their daily routine. The words
had to become muscle memory in the same way that everyone
learns to play a musical instrument, perform a dance, or train
for a sport. The verses at 6 Deuteronomy 1–9 laid out how the
Torah was to stay enshrined in human bodies, minds, hearts,
and spirits, in human interactions, and in physical spaces.

These are the commands, decrees and laws
the Lord your God directed me to teach you to observe
in the land
that you are crossing the Jordan to possess,
so that you, your children and their children after them
may fear the Lord your God as long as you live
by keeping all his decrees and commands that I give you,
and so that you may enjoy long life....
These commandments that I give you today are to be on
your hearts.
Impress them on your children.
Talk about them when you sit at home
and when you walk along the road,
when you lie down and when you get up.
Tie them as symbols on your hands and bind them on
your foreheads.
Write them on the doorframes of your houses and on
your gates.

Here is how Bible students committed and still commit the scriptures to muscle memory, according to theologian Ivan Illich.

> The process ... is typically Jewish rather than Greek ... memorization of this one book was performed by a process which stands in stark contrast to building of memory palaces (an imaginative mnemonic device used by Greek and Roman orators). The book was swallowed and digested through the careful attention paid to the psychomotor nerve impulses which accompany the sentences being learned. Even today, pupils in Koranic and Jewish schools sit on the floor with the book open on their knees. Each one chants his lines in a singsong, often a dozen simultaneously, each a different line. While they read, their bodies sway from the hips up or their trunks gently rock back and forth. The swinging and the recitation continue as if the student is in a trance, even when he closes his eyes or looks down the aisle of the mosque. The body movements re-evoke those of the speech organs that have been associated with them. In a ritual manner these students use their whole bodies to embody the lines.[2]

Muscle memory lasts much longer than other kinds of memory. That is why adults who learn to ride a bike as children can pick up a bike later and ride no matter how many years have passed. That's why seniors with dementia or memory loss can sing the songs and play the games they learned in childhood. First, physical muscle memory, or motor learning, occurs because muscles grow and store movements in their cells. Second, neurological memory results from motor learning stored in the central nervous system. Physical learning makes the brain and spinal cord change because it creates efficient and durable neural pathways to transmit the signals to the various parts of the body that need activation. With muscle memory, the brain no longer takes charge of remembering; the body takes over and movement is automatic. Rote learning has some surprising benefits for spirituality because words cease to be words and become lived experience and inner wisdom, perhaps a fusion of knowing/unknowing. Sacred passages turn into body prayers still recalled years later. Although I have not attended a Lutheran church for decades, I can still recite the liturgy, hymns, and prayers from memory. However, that knowing/unknowing can be hard won.

Hugh Brody, growing up in a Jewish home in England not long after World War II, described his experience learning the Hebrew language and scriptures at a neighborhood Hebrew school. He remembered that

> we learned Hebrew letters and recited, in Hebrew and English, sections of the Old Testament. The teachers ... were dour and pedantic, requiring the children to repeat and learn in the poorest forms of rote. We were given lines of Hebrew, then the translations into lines of English. We recited them, one after the other, over and over. Our teachers did their best to explain words, and I remember them explaining, with as much weary repetition as we brought to our recitations, the significance of sacred texts. Yet the meanings escaped me. The Hebrew seemed to have so little to do with the English: I failed to grasp that each bit of the one language had a translation in the other.[3]

Brody's experience with rote memorization is like what many others report. We do not like to practice skills and form habits to learn, and therefore modern educational methods are creative and innovative. We resist rote drills and practice, and yet, reading teachers have rediscovered the need for children to learn and practice basic reading skills. Everyone needs a set of quick automatic habits and strategies that do not place demands on our mental attention, so that our minds comprehend the message. Rote practice is necessary to become proficient at speaking and comprehending a foreign language, playing a musical instrument, and excelling at a sport. And yet Brody described how his childhood experiences of Hebrew had surprising spiritual benefits:

> As I prepared my bar mitzvah recital and learned to sing those lines of the Torah, I was fascinated by the tiny diacritics that encoded the changes in pitch and length, making words into something between incantation and song. Hebrew seemed to be full of magic.... [T]hinking back, I suspect that the magic of Hebrew ... had to do with an origin of meaning: which is to say no more than is said by many Orthodox Hebrew theologians and scholars. They have asserted—indeed, have depended upon the belief—that the *aleph-beis*, the alphabet of Hebrew is the "protoplasm of the universe", the very origin of divine authority and human spiritual experience. The theological view insists that the importance of Hebrew is something other and deeper than what its letters and words might mean as items of mere communication. This is a puzzling idea, yet it does reflect, if not explain, how I first experienced Hebrew. And the Jewish sages were no doubt conscious of what they were doing when they decided that the mystery of Hebrew could be sustained by retaining the complexity of its written form.[4]

To Brody and many others who have studied them through the centuries, the alphabet is the mysterious and mystical origin of the Word, and Torah words, incantations and songs are mystical carriers of Divine Wisdom. If lectio divina is a Quaker way of "eating the scroll," then such internalization of wisdom can lead us to the Divine Mystery of *being*, the peace and the love that comes from knowing by unknowing. Merton wrote, "Wisdom teaches us to experience the hidden realities of the mysteries of God by love, to enter into the world of divine things, in the peace of God that surpasses all understanding, and to 'know' divine things by the embrace of love in 'unknowing.'"[5]

Endnotes

1   Cranmore, Thomas, "Homily on the Reading of Scripture," Retrieved 11/11/2023 from http://www.anglicanlibrary. org/homilies/bk1hom01.htm

2   Illich, Ivan, *In the Vineyard of the Text*. University of Chicago Press. 1993, p. 60.

3   Brody, Hugh, *The Other Side of Eden: Hunters, Farmers, and the Shaping of the World*, Farrar, Straus, and Giroux, 2000, p. 68.

4   Brody, Hugh, *The Other Side of Eden: Hunters, Farmers, and the Shaping of the World*, Farrar, Straus, and Giroux, 2000, p. 69.

5   Merton, Thomas, "Lectio Divina," *Cistercian Studies Quarterly*, 50.1 2015, pp. 5–37.

Chapter 6

Praying the Scriptures

The sacred texts were meant to appeal to a person's hunger for things relational in nature: for forgiveness, grace, acceptance, and love. So the phrase is often used, "praying the scriptures," which refers to this engagement with God in prayer using the scriptures as an imaginative prayer tool.

David Baker

Sacred passages can be static words on a page in a forgotten book on a dusty shelf, or, as David Baker put it in his dissertation,[1] they can be a dynamic prayer tool to forge an intimate relation with Spirit and receive the gifts of the relation: forgiveness, grace, acceptance and love. By using their capacity for imagination and visualization, faithful readers make the stories reveal their secrets and relate to their lives. Filling in the missing details around Bible passages makes the words live in the present day. For instance, the New Testament says little about the life of Jesus. There is controversy about whether Jesus was literate or illiterate, because peasant boys like Jesus would not ordinarily have learned to read. Modern Christians cannot imagine how Jesus could have preached the way he did without knowing how to read. However, illiterate people are highly intelligent and capable, so I imagine that Jesus was well educated in the Torah and rabbinic commentaries even if he could not read the scrolls. What was Jesus like? For one thing, he was multilingual, a native speaker of Aramaic, along with Hebrew, some Greek and possibly some Latin.

When Alexander the Great (356–323 BCE), the king of Macedon, conquered the Persian Empire around 330 BCE, koiné

Greek served as the lingua franca in the Eastern Mediterranean. There was a triglossic situation, with Aramaic and koiné Greek as common spoken and written languages and Hebrew as the sacred language among educated Jews. By the time Jesus was born, literacy and proximity to Hebrew scripture had elevated the priests and scholars of the second (rebuilt) Temple to an exalted status. The Torah scrolls had become objects of veneration, as sacred as the wisdom they contained.

In those days, priestly scribes hand-copied the scrolls from another scroll or by dictation, and manual fabrication meant the sacred verses evolved to meet the needs of societies at the time. Intensive midrash continued in Hebrew, Aramaic, and koiné Greek at the Temple and at local synagogues. The term *synagogue*, from koiné Greek, refers to a place of assembly that functioned as a school, court, hostel, charity fund, and meeting place for the town. The early synagogues of the Galilee were monotheistic spaces where men and boys worshipped, studied, discussed, and prayed. The remains of as many as fifty different synagogues were identified in Galilee.[2]

The debate about Jesus's literacy misses the point that the sacred words of the Torah still thrived inside human hearts and memory. The culture at the time of Jesus was based on speaking and listening because most individuals could not read or write. In synagogues, Jews heard the Hebrew scriptures read aloud, and many boys and men could engage in midrash in Aramaic while still technically illiterate. Given his interest in all things spiritual, Jesus probably participated actively at a local synagogue, and experienced the scriptures viscerally as the Word of God. I like to think that Jesus consumed the scrolls. If so, there is a basis to understand a puzzling story about Jesus's childhood.

The story has it that when Jesus was twelve years old, his family went to the Passover festival in Jerusalem, and afterwards, his family left without him, thinking he was with some other families traveling together with them. When they could not find him, they went back to Jerusalem and after three days they found him "in the temple courts, sitting among the teachers, listening to them and asking them questions. Everyone who heard him was amazed at his understanding and his answers." When his parents found him there, they were surprised, but they were more upset about the inconvenience than about his participation in midrash. Like any mother, Mary complained about having to come back and look for him. Jesus said, "Why were you searching for me?" He asked, "Didn't you know I would be about my Father's business?"(Luke 2:4–52).

Jesus could have learned the Hebrew scriptures by heart and engaged in midrash in his local synagogue, so that he would be able to ask questions and understand the answers at the temple in Jerusalem. Or Jesus could have learned how to read the Hebrew scriptures himself. If he learned how to read on his own, perhaps he did it ingeniously like Frederick Douglass, who learned a little from his slaveowner and then tricked literate white boys into teaching him what they knew. Either way, the story concludes, "Jesus grew in wisdom and stature, and in favor with God and man." Either option would explain how an undistinguished carpenter preached eloquently and cited verses from scripture in his ministry.

A story told in 4 Luke 16–22 tells about a time when Jesus read from a scroll in the synagogue in his hometown of Nazareth as a literacy test in the synagogue. Scrolls did not have typographic conventions like chapters, numbers, verses, or indexes, and they were clumsy, so it would have been hard to find a specific text (6 Isaiah 1) quickly. However, Jesus found the right passage in the scroll and read it despite the difficulty, or else he knew the Isaiah prophecies so well that he simply recited the relevant passage while pretending to find it in the scroll.

He went to Nazareth, where he had been brought up, and
on the Sabbath day he went into the synagogue, as
was his custom. He stood up to read, and the scroll of
the prophet Isaiah was handed to him. Unrolling it, he
found the place where it is written:
"The Spirit of the Lord is on me, because he has anointed me
to proclaim good news to the poor.
He has sent me to proclaim freedom for the prisoners
and recovery of sight for the blind,
to set the oppressed free,
to proclaim the year of the Lord's favor."
Then he rolled up the scroll, gave it back to the attendant
and sat down. The eyes of everyone in the synagogue
were fastened on him. He began by saying to them,
"Today this scripture is fulfilled in your hearing."
All spoke well of him and were amazed at the gracious
words that came from his lips. "Isn't this Joseph's
son?" they asked.

Nevertheless, at the end of the story, the people rejected Jesus,
and he said, "No prophet is accepted in his hometown." There is
a contrasting yet similar story in 6 Mark, in which Jesus, again in
Nazareth, began to preach in the synagogue. This congregation
was offended and questioned his abilities because they knew
Jesus only as an unassuming man like them, not especially
learned or wise. "Where did this man get these things?" they
asked. "What's this wisdom that has been given him? What
are these remarkable miracles he is performing? Isn't this
the carpenter? Isn't this Mary's son and the brother of James,
Joseph, Judas and Simon? Aren't his sisters here with us?" And
they took offense at him. Jesus said to them, "A prophet is not
without honor except in his own town, among his relatives and
in his own home."

It is unclear how these stories,[3] with their similar conclusions, relate to each other, but they imply that although Jesus was not an especially educated man, he was knowledgeable about the scripture and wise in his preaching. His ability to minister and teach was remarkable. He impressed some Nazarenes and infuriated others. They resented him and begrudged his wisdom; his message of hope and freedom for the poor and oppressed threatened their status. I prefer to imagine Jesus as a humble self-taught sage carrying his sacred wisdom like a flame in his heart memory.

In a later story in Luke, the Transfiguration story, wisdom transformed Jesus (9 Luke 28–30). Jesus went up into a mountain to pray, taking a few disciples with him. How did Jesus pray? The text does not say because it assumes that listeners/readers know how to pray. I can visualize the details. He prayed like the prophets of the Hebrew Bible, rocking his body back and forth, ruminating on the sacred words in his heart. He may have chanted a beautiful verse from 61 Isaiah 11 as a mantra: "For as the soil makes the sprout come up and a garden causes seeds to grow, so the LORD will make righteousness and praise spring up before all nations."

Slowly, Jesus quieted his own fearful thoughts and centered his mind, until he experienced union with *being*. In a vision or a visualization, Jesus saw his heroes, Moses and Elijah, who revealed his future death at Jerusalem. In this story, Jesus and his disciples experienced bright lights, glory, clouds, and a heavenly voice identifying Jesus as a child of Spirit.

Such stories about Jesus circulated mouth to ear to mouth and those who formed the Jesus Movement after Jesus's death learned them by heart. Acts 4:13 says that Jesus's followers were unschooled, ordinary people. Everything we know about Jesus and his ministry was in the memories of his unlettered disciples. The Jesus stories often referred to the Hebrew Bible and the allusions added depth, nuance, imagination, and explanation to the teachings. For instance, in 11 Matthew 18–19, Jesus preached about people's unrepentance and hardheartedness, and spoke about himself self-deprecatingly. "For John came neither eating nor drinking, and they say, 'He has a demon.' The Child of Humanity came eating and drinking, and they say, 'Here is a glutton and a drunkard, a friend of tax collectors and sinners.' But Wisdom Sophia is proved right by her deeds."

The final line may be cryptic to modern readers, or a non sequitur. *Sophia*, the embodiment of Wisdom in Greek, is the Divine Feminine called *Chokmah* in the Hebrew Bible. Sophia/Chokmah describes herself in a beautiful passage at 8 Proverbs. Thus, for Jesus's listeners and for Matthew's readers in later years, the name Sophia points directly to Proverbs 9, just like a footnote of today. Sophia/Chokmah was a wild woman who flouted norms of female modesty to prophesize by the main gate, and her wisdom is vindicated by her unexpected deeds.

> Does not wisdom call out?
> Does not understanding raise her voice?
> At the highest point along the way,
> where the paths meet, she takes her stand;
> beside the gate leading into the city,
> at the entrance, she cries aloud:
> "To you, O people, I call out;
> I raise my voice to all mankind.
> You who are simple, gain prudence;
> you who are foolish, set your hearts on it.
> Listen, for I have trustworthy things to say;
> I open my lips to speak what is right.
> My mouth speaks what is true,
> for my lips detest wickedness.
> All the words of my mouth are just;
> none of them is crooked or perverse.

As the stories of Jesus and his teachings were repeated by mouth, they were altered, as is normal with orally transmitted knowledge. Decades passed between the time Jesus walked on earth and the stories were written down, perhaps during CE 50–100. When literate believers authored stories, parables, and sermons, they used koiné Greek. Each gospel was a separate entity, not related to any other, which is why there are so many disparities among them. Divergences did not matter because each early Christian community had its preferred texts while others had others. It was only later that some, but not all, early Christian writings were collected into the New Testament, and we read and compared them.

The Jesus Movement spread to neighboring cities and nations, including to Rome. Romans used wax tablets to write, and wax tablets led to a different technology, the codex, which replaced the scroll for most purposes.[4] A codex was composed of vellum, parchment, skin, or papyrus sheets sewn together on one side like books. Codices were more advanced than bulky scrolls because they opened flat and allowed for writing on both sides. Proto-Christians embraced the new compact codex technology; the Nag Hammadi texts are leather-bound papyrus codices.

Still, the need for the faithful to eat and digest the sacred texts remained. The Book of Revelation was written down for the first time around the year CE 96, though it refers to events that occurred earlier. The author, John, warned about the dangers of codifying sacred words in static print and leaving them on the shelf and not in the heart, referencing the same scroll image as in Ezekial in Revelation 10: 8–11.

Then the voice that I had heard from heaven spoke to me
    once more:
"Go, take the scroll that lies open in the hand of the angel
who is standing on the sea and on the land."

> So I went to the angel and asked him to give me the little
>   scroll.
> He said to me, "Take it and eat it. It will turn your stomach
>   sour,
> but in your mouth it will be as sweet as honey."
> I took the little scroll from the angel's hand and ate it.
> It tasted as sweet as honey in my mouth,
> but when I had eaten it, my stomach turned sour.
> Then I was told, "You must prophesy again
> about many peoples, nations, languages and kings."

The angel warned John that the wisdom would taste sweet and yet it could cause discomfort to him and to those he preached to. This was what Jesus experienced in Nazareth; knowing/ unknowing both gives and takes away. It puts us through the refiner's fire [3 Malachi], and it restores us to wholesomeness and humility, opening us to the plight of others. Thomas Kelly called this paradox *contemptus mundi* — when Friends are painfully "torn away from earthly attachments and ambitions" and at the same time, *amor mundi*, we are "quickened to a divine but painful concern for the world." According to Kelly, we become not of this world and yet the world becomes our beloved concern. The Light of Christ "plucks the world out of our hearts, loosening the chains of attachment. And He hurls the world into our hearts, where we and He together carry it in infinitely tender love."[5] John's story makes it clear that eating the scroll has consequences, hard-won self-knowledge on the one hand, and prophecy and leadership on the other.

The Divine told John to prophesize, not just to the house of Israel, but to many nations, languages, and kingdoms. This was a change from the earlier eat-a-scroll story in Ezekial and the isolationist story of the Tower of Babel from Genesis, where God deliberately confounded human cooperation for all time by interfering and causing communities to speak different languages instead of a common one. Now, the Divine wanted believers to cooperate and live in peace, preaching to anyone who would listen, in any nation and in many languages. To accomplish this mission, Spirit enabled them to speak other tongues according to 2 Acts 1–4. Spirit gathered them, filled them, and taught them to minister and listen in tongues. If only Friends could learn to speak and understand different spiritual languages as easily.

When the day of Pentecost came, they were all together
    in one place.
Suddenly a sound like the blowing of a violent wind
    came from heaven
and filled the whole house where they were sitting.
They saw what seemed to be tongues of fire that separated
and came to rest on each of them.
All of them were filled with the Holy Spirit
and began to speak in other tongues as the Spirit enabled
    them.

Endnotes

1   Baker, David, "Lectio Divina: Towards a Psychology of Contemplation," PH.D. dissertation, Pacifica Graduate Institute, 2002

2   "Early Synagogues in Galilee," Retrieved 10/1/2023 from https://whc.unesco.org/en/tentativelists/1470/.

3   This is one of the very few stories to appear in each gospel (Matthew 13:54–58, Mark 6:1–6, Luke 4:16–30, John 4:44) with a similar final statement from Jesus. See "How Do Mark 6:1–6 and Luke 4:16–30 Compare?" Retrieved 11/11/2023 from https://hermeneutics.stackexchange.com/questions/85042/how-do-mark-61-6-and-luke-416-30-compare

4   Torah scrolls are kept in cabinets called arks in modern synagogues.

5   Kelly, Thomas, *A Testament of Devotion*, Harper Collins Publishing, 1941, p. 47

Chapter 7

Reading in the Monasteries

Whenever [Francis] read the Sacred Books, and something was once tossed into his mind, he indelibly wrote it on his heart. He had a memory for [whole] books because having heard something once he took it in not idly but with continued devout attentions, his emotion-memory [affectus] chewed on it.

Brother Thomas Celano

Franciscan monk Thomas of Celano (1185–1260), the biographer of St. Francis (c. 1181–1226), wrote that Francis preferred memorizing and ruminating on sacred words to discussing theology or philosophy.[1] Lectio divina engaged his affect, his sensibilities, in a way that logic and reason did not. However, long before the time of St. Francis, nuns and monks retreated to isolated communities to ruminate on scriptures far from worldly distractions. One early Jesus follower, Eusebius Hieronymus, better known as Jerome (347–420), left Europe in the fourth century and settled in Bethlehem, founding a monastery where he translated the Hebrew Bible into Latin. He learned Hebrew so that he could work from the original scriptures after learning that the Greek version, called the Septuagint, was not accurate. His Vulgate Bible remained the standard Bible in western Europe until the sixteenth century, when translations in European vernacular languages were published. That is the Bible that St. Francis inscribed on his heart with devout attention.

By the fifth century CE, Latin was the standard liturgical and scriptural language in Western Europe, and most monks had to learn Latin as a second language through traditional study methods like dictation and psychomotor memorization.

> The teacher pronounced each syllable separately, and the pupils repeated in a chorus of syllables and words. As the teacher dictates to the pupil, the pupil dictates to his own hand. The *deogratias* which was a familiar [spoken] utterance now takes on the shape of two successive words [in writing]. The single words of Latin impress themselves as a sequence of syllables on the ear of the pupil. They become part of his sense of touch, which remembers how the hand moved to cut them in the wax. They appear as visible traces which impress themselves on the sense of sight. Lips and ears, hands and eyes conspire in shaping the pupil's memory for the Latin words.[2]

Over the decades, the dialects of spoken Latin became European romance languages, leaving Classical Latin as a lingua franca among clergy and educated elites in Europe. Now, the Roman liturgy no longer uses Latin, but it is the official language of the Holy See, the government of the Roman church although Italian is its main working language.[3]

St. Benedict of Nursia (CE 480–547) founded monastic communities in Italy and devised a Rule around 530 that monks and nuns still follow. The Rule established a habit of prayer which came later to be known by its Latin name, lectio divina. Lectio divina was never silent and solitary; from the beginning it was communal instruction with exegesis, meditation, and contemplation. For centuries, monks and nuns met in their chapels seven times ("Offices") a day to listen to recitations from sacred texts, chant, and sing. Between the Offices, they mumbled what they remembered from the sacred texts in their own way, called *ora et labora* [work and pray], as they went about their day. The mumbled repetitive verses always kept them in a state of divine accompaniment, blurring any distinction between prayer and work. "For the monk, lectio divina, the reading of sacred texts, is a central part of the rhythm of the day, as a kind of reading which engages the whole body.... [R]eading is not simply a single activity but a way of life for as the monk follows the particular rule throughout the course of a day, he reads along the way."[4]

Karen Armstrong wrote that lectio divina "does not refer primarily to the pious perusal of 'spiritual books', but rather to a technique of prayer. It is a means of descending to the level of the heart where, in the Christian tradition, one finds God."[5] In the cloisters, nuns and monks did not prize novelty over familiarity, and they recited and prayed the same passages repeatedly. This is true for children and infants too; they prefer to hear the same stories over and over again until they know them by heart and can "read" the story by looking at the pictures. Sister Jean Chittister described her experience this way,

The number of times the community prays together over and over every day in every monastery is not the true value of the exercise. The purpose of communal prayer is to read the psalms and the scriptures together over and over every day in every monastery until they sink into our souls like the air we breathe. It is the daily, drip, drip, drip of the scriptures into the hearts and minds of every member of the community—years after those scriptures were gathered and formed into books—that forms the soul and heart of the monastic.[6]

Earlier Hebrew and proto-Christian prophets described their prayer using the metaphor of eating and swallowing holy words, and so did these monks and nuns. To them, lectio divina meant chewing the codices and ruminating on their contents through physical movements of the mouth, subvocalizing the words. "A monk spent two to three hours each day in lectio divina ("divine study"). He would imagine himself standing beside Moses on Sinai or at the foot of Jesus's cross. Instead of simply running his eyes over the page, he would mouth the words, murmuring them subvocally, a practice recommended by classical rhetoricians as an aid to memorization."[7]

Nowadays, psycholinguists know that subvocalizing or pronouncing words quietly is a good way to learn because it uses the sound and muscle memory to store words and phrases for later retrieval.

> Monks compared lectio divina literally to a cow's rumination—a metaphor possibly suggested by the "chewing" movement of the mouth. Memory was the stomach and scripture, the sweet-smelling cud that, ingested, became a part of himself and, when required, could be recalled from the stomach to the palate and spoken aloud. The text, therefore, became integral to the monk. A good monk ... will devour and digest the holy books ... because their memory does not let go of the rules of life.... The whisper of lectio became the voice of meditation....[8]

Mumbling prayers in lectio divina quiets the left hemisphere of the brain, the narrative voice or "monkey mind," and allows the more intuitive and emotional right hemisphere to operate more fully, as mantras do in meditation.

However, recall that, from early on in the history of the written scripture, there were two "orientations" in the practice of sacred reading and writing. Alongside reading as a form of prayer, the tradition of exegesis persisted in synagogues and monasteries. In the monasteries, one orientation was "monastic lectio" and the other was "scholastic lectio" or study and interpretation. Baker differentiated the two:

Both reference an activity that is "holy" *sacra,* divina; but within the two spheres, the emphasis is put on two distinct aspects of the same activity. The procedure is different because the beginning orientation is different. The *scholastic lectio* takes the direction of the *quaestio* [questioning] and the *disputatio* [rhetorical disputation]. The reader puts questions to the text and then questions himself on the subject matter.... The monastic lectio is oriented toward the *meditatio* [meditation] and the *oratio* [prayer].[9]

Exegetical reading was, like most modern reading, left-brained by its very nature. It tended to be analytical and critical, and it required novelty and innovation. Scholars used reasoning and logic to write and read arguments in scripture and commentaries. In the eleventh century, a monk named Anselm of Canterbury (1033–1109) developed an ontological proof that God existed, using logical arguments based on Greek philosophy. The details of his proof are not important; the proof shows that scholastic reading was becoming more modern in nature. Lectio divina continued as always, but highly educated monks began to seek religious truth in the Bible, not consolation, inspiration, and prayer. For these monks, reading scripture was less and less an imaginative prayer tool.

Around the same time (in the cloisters and the wider culture) silent solitary reading began to be a habitual behavior. Prior to this, monastic reading was oral, communal, internally directed, and local in its effects, but scholastic reading soon became externally focused, and widespread in its effects because scholastics published the results of study for others outside the monastery to read. Scholars tried to write more accurate translations of the Bible and made line by line commentaries. The literate culture at the time had no sharp division between the religious and the secular.

Medieval scholastics did not distinguish between knowledge of the natural world that could derive from science on the one hand and sacred wisdom that derived from scripture on the other. They looked into the Bible with critical eyes to find logic and history.

William of Ockham (1285–1349) an English Franciscan (of Ockham's razor fame) insisted that "doctrinal statements are literally true and should be subjected to stringent rational enquiry."[10] The same rigid thinking was applied to the printed scriptures. Carefully handprinted and illustrated codices, true artforms created with devotion, gave way to plainer block-printed and bound books made without the embellishment or devotion. Then, in 1452, Gutenberg used a modified grape press and moveable type to produce around 180 copies of the Vulgate Bible on vellum. The meaning of the word "manufacture" "make by hand" changed to "make by machine."

Still, many people did not know Latin, and most Europeans, especially women, were illiterate, so they could not read and understand the Bible themselves. The Roman hierarchy, through the priests, mediated between the Divine and ordinary folk in the church. The Reformation changed this status quo. In 1522, Luther's New Testament in German appeared, and the first edition of the whole Bible was published in 1534. The Tyndale Bible in English and the more complete Coverdale Bible appeared by 1535. Finally able to read the Bible, many Christians saw that there were important contradictions between different books of the Bible, between various verses of the Bible and, more importantly perhaps, between the Bible and what science was uncovering. Furthermore, Bibles were affordable and transportable, so the urgent need to memorize and internalize the texts evaporated.

What had still been primarily an oral/aural culture turned into a culture of print for the growing number of literate individuals. Within a brief time, they realized that it was much easier to read printed books than handwritten books because the margins were even and the font was uniform, albeit ornate. Editors added organization and page numbers. They started identifying Bible verses by chapter and verse. Printed pages looked reasonable, logical, and even scientific, and for the first time, print gave the impression of a truthfulness which readers could question or defend.

Scholastic reading and the culture of readily available printed books resulted in existential questions: How could the Bible, the inspired word of God, be wrong? Can the world be both religious and secular at the same time? Can faith and science co-exist as Truth? Priests and authorities pressured the laity to choose one or the other, and so the tensions between types of truth, subjective/objective, scriptural/ scientific, and heartfelt/ cognitive, began. The more threatened believers felt, the more they wanted the Bible to be the literal words of God. In this new left-brained world, there was little middle ground, there was no room for imagination, visualization, and metaphor. For many, the concept of the omniscient father God high in the sky triumphed and the creation story of Genesis went from myth to literal truth. For others, it was easier to fall away and (privately) declare the inefficacy of the Divine, religious beliefs, and prayer.

Still, lectio divina continued as a practice among monks and nuns in monasteries and among a few lay people in the world. Although there is no direct reference to monastic reading among the first generation of Friends, they did read deeply and devotionally with Spirit within. Early Friend Isaac Penington (1616–79) described that way of reading when he wrote, "And the end of words is to bring men to the knowledge of things beyond what words can utter. So, learn of the Lord to make a right use of the Scriptures: which is by esteeming them in their right place, and prizing that above them which is above them."[11]

Endnotes

1   Armstrong, Karen, *The Lost Art of Scripture: Rescuing the Sacred Texts*, Knopf 2019. p. 302.

2   Illich, Ivan, *In the Vineyard of the Text*, University of Chicago Press. 1990, p. 70.

3   Languages of Vatican City. Retrieved 9/9/2023 from https://en.wikipedia.org/wiki/Languages_of_Vatican City.

4   Baker, David, *Lectio Divina: Toward a Psychology of Contemplation*, Pacific Graduate Institute 2002, pp. 65–66.

5   Armstrong, Karen, *The Lost Art of Scripture: Rescuing the Sacred Texts*, Knopf 2019, p. 296.

6   Chittister, Joan, *The Monastic Heart: 50 Simple Practices for a Contemplative and Fulfilling Life*, Convergent Books, 2021, p. 41.

7   Armstrong, Karen, *The Lost Art of Scripture: Rescuing the Sacred Texts*, Knopf 2019, p. 297, citing medieval author Hugh of Fouilloy.

8   Armstrong, Karen, *The Lost Art of Scripture: Rescuing the Sacred Texts*, Knopf 2019, p. 297, citing medieval author Hugh of Fouilloy.

9   Baker, David, *Lectio Divina: Toward a Psychology of Contemplation*, Pacifica Graduate Institute, 2002, p. 60.

10 Armstrong, Karen, *The Lost Art of Scripture: Rescuing the Sacred Texts*, Knopf, 2019, p. 308.

11 Penington Isaac, cited in Macy, Howard. "Quakers and Scripture" in *The Oxford Handbook of Quaker Studies* ed. by Stephen W. Angell and Ben Pink Dandelion. Oxford University 2015. Retrieved 9/30/2023 from https://digitalcommons.georgefox.edu/ccs/213/.

Chapter 8

Understanding from Within

> We can go back into that Life within whom Amos and Isaiah lived, that Life in God's presence and vivid guidance, when we understand the writings from within. For we and Isaiah and Hosea feed on the same Life, are rooted in the same holy flame which is burning in our hearts.
>
> **Thomas Kelly**[1]

The first generation of Friends believed that the same Spirit who revealed the scriptures acted within them as the Light of Christ. They received spiritual guidance and experienced Divine Presence through reading, understanding, and writing about the scriptures and other spiritual texts. While they recognized the authority of the Bible as a guide, they emphasized spiritual transformation through personal revelation triggered by reading the Bible. In the 1940s, Thomas Kelly thought that Quakers had "a special approach" to the Bible, one that was very like lectio divina. Kelly meant that Friends could approach and enter the prophetic lives of biblical prophets if they, with empathy and imagination, felt the same holy flame burning in their hearts. By reading the Bible from within, early Quakers navigated a middle but sometimes contentious ground between belief in the word-for-word inerrancy of the Bible and scientific rejection of the Bible. Wilmer Cooper wrote that

> Early Friends immersed themselves in the Bible, which was so much a part of their religious culture that its authority was taken for granted. It was said of George Fox that were the Scriptures lost, he could reconstruct

them from memory. Whether or not this was true, he and other Friends were not only familiar with the Bible but took it seriously as a religious guide for their life.[2] While they read the words in the Bible they hoped and prayed to experience direct revelation of the Word. George Fox wrote about an experience in 1647, "For though I read the Scriptures that spake of Christ and of God, yet I knew Him not but by revelation, as He who hath the key did open, and as the father of life drew me to His Son by His Spirit."[3]

The history of Friends and the Bible goes back to the very beginning of the first translations to the English language. In 1560, English-speaking Puritan refugees in Switzerland commissioned the Geneva Bible. Printed later in England with permission from Queen Elizabeth, English readers with the money to buy it could purchase the Bible for the first time. The Geneva Bible came with study guides and citations so that readers could cross-reference verses, book introductions, an index, as well as maps, tables, and illustrations. Some of this material was politically radical.[4] It was the primary Bible for sixteenth-century English-speaking Protestant sects and Pilgrims carried copies to America on the Mayflower. The King James Version, published in 1611, was meant to counteract the Puritan slant of the Geneva Bible in favor of the Church of England. George Fox recommended that the New Testament be translated into every language and showed interest in comparing the various English versions available to him.[5] Early Friends took the middle path by using both the Geneva Bible and the King James Bible.[6]

During the English Civil War (1642–1651), Oliver Cromwell's soldiers were issued a passport-sized version of the Geneva Bible called *The Souldiers Pocket Bible*,[7] which contained around 150 war-related verses intended as propaganda to inspire morale and indoctrination to reinforce discipline. Typical verses were 20 Deuteronomy 4 "For the Lord your God goeth with you, to fight for you against your enemies, and to save you." and 14 Exodus 14 "The Lord shall fight for you." There is a classic anecdote about lifesaving scripture, that a soldier's life was spared when the Bible in a pocket near his heart stopped a bullet. As far as I was able to confirm, this was the first time (but not the last) that military leaders gave soldiers portable scriptures during wartime, and since then, the story about the life-saving Bible has taken on a life of its own. According to Cromwell, his soldiers never lost a battle after the pocket Bible was issued to them in 1643. Since many Quaker men came from Oliver Cromwell's New Model Army, it is interesting to speculate on this experience of biblical propaganda and indoctrination, and the subsequent declarations of the peace testimony based on passages like 5 Matthew 38–46 (which references verses from the Hebrew Bible).

You have heard that it was said, "Eye for eye, and tooth for tooth." But I tell you, do not resist an evil person. If anyone slaps you on the right cheek, turn to them the other cheek also. And if anyone wants to sue you and take your shirt, hand over your coat as well. If anyone forces you to go one mile, go with them two miles. Give to the one who asks you, and do not turn away from the one who wants to borrow from you. You have heard that it was said, "Love your neighbor and hate your enemy." But I tell you, love your enemies and pray for those who persecute you, that you may be children of your Father in heaven. He causes his sun to rise on the evil and the good, and sends rain on the righteous and the unrighteous. If you love those who love you, what reward will you get? Are not even the tax collectors doing that?

Like proto-Christian New Testament writers, Fox and other early Friends used Bible passages to reinforce their religious views. In his writings, Fox made many allusions to lend weight, legitimacy, and authority to his point of view. His modern editors insert the references in square brackets for us modern Bible illiterates. One of my favorites is Fox's Epistle 10. When I first came across Epistle 10, the citations that editors added inside brackets were annoying disruptions that I did not understand and when I copied the text by hand into my journal, I skipped them. Later, when I took the time to look up the verses in the Bible, they added nuance and context to Fox's message. So it is with a lot of early Quaker writings; the acknowledged or unacknowledged allusions to the Bible add a rich texture of meaning that passes many modern readers by.

> To Friends, to stand still in trouble, and see the strength of the Lord.
> Friends—Whatever ye are addicted to, the tempter will come in that thing; and when he can trouble you, then he gets advantage over you [2 Cor 2:11], and then ye are gone.
> Stand still in that which is pure, after ye see yourselves; and then mercy comes in.
> After thou seest thy thoughts, and the temptations, do not think, but submit; and then power comes.
> Stand still in that which shows and discovers; and there doth strength immediately come.
> And stand still in the light, and submit to it, and the other will be hushed and gone;
> and then content comes.
> And when temptations and troubles appear, sink down in that which is pure,
> and all will be hushed, and fly away.

Your strength is to stand still, after ye see yourselves;
    whatsoever ye see yourselves addicted to, temptations,
    corruption, uncleanness, &c. then ye think ye shall
    never overcome.
And earthly reason will tell you, what ye shall lose;
    hearken not to that, but stand still in the light that
    shows them to you, and then strength comes from the
    Lord, and help contrary to your expectation.
Then ye grow up in peace, and no trouble shall move you.
David fretted himself, when he looked out [Eccl 12:3];
but when he was still, no trouble could move him.
    [Psa 37:1,7f]
When your thoughts are out, abroad, then troubles move
    you.
But come to stay your minds upon that spirit [Isa 26:3]
    which was before the letter;
here ye learn to read the scriptures aright.
If ye do any thing in your own wills, then ye tempt God;
    but stand still in that power which brings peace.

Dean Freiday summarized the early Quaker view of the Bible, citing early Friend Robert Barclay's Apology.[8] Barclay knew many Bible passages by heart so he could easily include them in his writing without stopping to look them up. God was his "good Remembrancer." Barclay noted that he had to omit some useful citations because he could not immediately recall them. According to Freiday, "Even more remarkable than Barclay's inspired memory was the organization of his citations. Often only a brief phase was used from one book of the Bible, followed by a selection from another, or perhaps by another passage a dozen verses later. The transitions are so smooth and the logic so sequential that his editorial work is hardly noticeable."[9]

In his Proposition 3, Barclay held that the Bible contained a faithful historical account of God's chosen, prophetic accounts from the past and for the future, and a full adequate account of the principles and doctrines of Christ. He advised Friends to take the Bible as a gold standard in a special sense. Friends should test their testimonies by comparing them with the Bible and reject as false anything that contradicted the Bible. Freiday points out that the Bible never mentions a central Quaker testimony, continuing revelation, although it may be implicit. Continuing revelation means that the same inspiration for the Bible also reveals insights on "the matters for which the foundations have already been laid."[10] Quakers criticized Christians who made an idol of the Bible, displacing the Light of Christ. They themselves did not believe everything in the Bible; "while one tenth of Scripture contains the fundamental doctrines of the Christian religion, the rest is not pertinent or useless."[11]

Margaret Fell remembered her experience of one of Fox's sermons:

> You will say Christ saith this and the apostles say this, but what canst thou say? Art thou a child of the Light and hast thou walked in the Light, and what thou speakest, is it inwardly from God, etc.? This opened me so, that it cut me to the heart, and then I saw clearly that we were all wrong. So I sat me down in my pew again and cried bitterly: and I cried in my spirit to the Lord, we are all thieves, we are all thieves, we have taken the Scriptures in words, and know nothing of them in ourselves.[12]

Howard Macy summarizes the diverse points of view about the Bible in Quakerism in the centuries after the first generation of Friends, and it is not possible to do justice to that complex history here.[13] Among twentieth-century Friends, some minimize the Bible or ignore it altogether. Others engage with it frequently to encounter Spirit. Some Friends appreciate the Bible, and yet they prefer not to study it because study seems counter to Spirit. Still other Friends, often carrying negative childhood memories with them, run the other way when someone mentions the Bible. There is no unanimity about the Bible.

Many Friends credit Elias Hicks as a founder of modern liberal Quaker theology. Liberal unprogrammed Friends give preference to Spirit or Light over the Bible, following this advice from Elias Hicks in a sermon delivered in 1826.

> Here we see a beautiful path open to every man and woman; and so plain that the wayfaring man, though a fool, cannot err therein, when we come to the right thing, the Light which maketh it manifest; for we can get no right knowledge but through this Light. As we have need of the light of the outward sun in temporal things, so we must come to know the inward sun, the inward Light, to be that from which we must derive all knowledge of spiritual things, and all that relates to the soul and its nourishment—that which sustains and continues it alive in God, and which is the source of its happiness and joy.[14]

Still, although the Bible became less important, sacred reading and writing remained popular among unprogrammed Friends, and reading expanded to include texts from many other spiritual paths. In 1972, Douglas Steere wrote about Henry Hodgkin (1877–1933), founder of the Pendle Hill Center in Pennsylvania. He read and wrote voraciously, which made him a strong minister and spiritual adviser to others.

> One of the greatest Christians I ever knew was Henry T. Hodgkin.... He read widely and deeply and each morning of his adult life he spent an hour in religious concern—a third given to religious reading, a third to the exercise of prayer, and a third to writing in a journal or daybook. He

did not simply record the simple events that happened the previous day; rather he used the book to write his mind out on things that had come up in his prayer or reading or situations in which he was involved.

Steere linked Hodgkin's careful preparation and his prowess with ministry, writing,

> His strength in the ministry and as a counselor of human beings may have had little to do with this particular pattern of preparation and others may have very different ways of keeping close to the root, but I have never been able to shake off the conviction that Henry Hodgkin lived as a man who was prepared in private for life in public and that there was a connection between the two that was worth pondering.[15]

Hodgkin did not limit his reading to a narrow Biblical canon. He read the Bible and other sacred texts to spark his prayer, understanding, and revelation.

Overall, the balance among liberal unprogrammed Quakers has shifted towards accessing the Light and hoping for revelation and transformation through silence in worship, and not through sacred reading and writing as a spiritual practice. Nevertheless, there are some caveats about the quality of the silence in Meeting for Worship. Rufus Jones wrote,

> (The early Friends) made the discovery that silence is one of the best preparations for communion (with God) and for the reception of inspiration and guidance. Silence itself, of course, has no magic. It may be just sheer emptiness, absence of words or noise or music. It may be an occasion for slumber, or it may be a dead form. But it may be an intensified pause, a vitalised hush, a creative quiet, an

actual moment of mutual and reciprocal correspondence with God. The actual meeting of man with God and God with man is the very crown and culmination of what we can do with our human life here on earth.[16]

How can Friends help Meetings avoid emptiness, absence, or slumber in the silence? How can Friends prepare to receive inspiration and guidance, or contribute to a full and vital Gathering Presence in worship? Lectio divina is one way. A contemporary of Rufus Jones, Father Romano Guardini, a professor in Germany until the Nazis expelled him in 1939, wrote that lectio divina did not generate ideas for us to think about on the intellectual level. Instead, it plants seeds that, if received with openness and gratitude, will grow and fruit in the silence of Meeting for Worship. "It possesses the power of growth, the strength to start and develop life. Hence we must not receive it as we grasp an idea with our mind, but as earth receives a grain of wheat."[17]

Endnotes

1   Kelly, Thomas, "The Quaker Discovery," in *The Eternal Promise*. Friends United Press, 2nd ed. 1988, p. 68–69.

2   Cooper, Wilmer, *A Living Faith: An Historical and Comparative Study of Quaker Beliefs*, Friends United Press, 1990

3   Newman, Henry S. ed., *The Autobiography of George Fox from his Journal*, 2nd ed. London: S. W. Partridge and Co., and Leominster: The Orphans' Printing Press, n.d. [Preface date, 1886])

4   Hardin, Craig, "The Geneva Bible as a Political Document," *Pacific Historical Review* Vol. 7, No. 1 1938, pp. 40–49.

5   Cadbury, Henry, "A Quaker Approach to the Bible." *Quaker Universalist Fellowship*. Retrieved 6/29/3023 from https://universalistfriends.org/cadbury-1.html

6   Worden, Ronald, "Text and Revelation-George Fox's Use of the Bible," *Quaker Religious Thought* Vol. 97, Article 3. 2001. p. 14.

7   *The Souldiers Bible* Retrieved 8/8/2023 from https://en.wikipedia.org/wiki/The_Souldiers Pocket Bible

8   Barclay, Robert, *Barclay's Apology in Modern English* ed. by Dean Freiday, Barclay Press, 4th printing, 1991.

9   Freiday, Dean, "Robert Barclay and Scripture," *Quaker Religious Thought* Vol. 97, Article 4. 2001. Available at: https://digitalcommons.georgefox.edu/qrt/vol97/iss1/4

10   Barclay, Robert, *Apology*, III, p. 64.

11   Barclay, Robert, *Apology*, III, p. 64.

12   Fell, Margaret, cited in Cadbury, Henry, "A Quaker Approach to the Bible," *Quaker Universalist Fellowship* Retrieved 6/29/3023 from https://universalistfriends.org/cadbury-1.html

13   Macy, Howard, "Quakers and Scripture" in *The Oxford Handbook of Quaker Studies* ed. by Stephen W. Angell and Ben Pink Dandelion. Oxford University 2015. Retrieved 9/30/2023 from https://digitalcommons.georgefox.edu/ccs/213/.

14   Hicks, Elias, "The Blood of Jesus A Sermon and Prayer Delivered at Darby Meeting," Philadelphia Yearly Meeting, 1826. *The Quaker*, Vol. I No. 1. Retrieved 11/1/2022 from http://www.qhpress.org/quakerpages/qhoa/hicksdarby.htm

15   Steere, Douglas, *On Speaking out of the Silence; Vocal Ministry in the Unprogrammed Meeting for Worship*, Pendle Hill #182, 1972, p.19.

16   Jones, Rufus, *Testimony of The Soul*, 1937. Whitefish: Kessinger Publishing, 2006. Retrieved 12/4/2022 From Https://Www.Fgcquaker.Org/Exercises/Friendly-Voices-6/

17   Guardini, Romano, *Meditations before Mass*, Sophia Institute Press, 1993, p. 66.

Chapter 9

Changing Lenses

> There are times when the Holy Spirit makes us
> keenly aware of the fact that no human analysis, no
> construction of a big theoretical system, no body of
> spiritual ideas or concepts is of deep and lasting
> value in the spiritual life, and that the divine
> realities which we hunger for by far exceed the
> power of words, thoughts, and theories to contain.
>
> **Thomas Merton**[1]

Early Friends advocated a middle way of reading sacred texts
remarkably close to what Merton described as lectio divina.
Sacred words and concepts only point readers towards a reality
of *being*. The historical context and meaning of sacred passages
are important, especially when scribes have succumbed to
the temptation to alter scripture to suit their own prejudices.
The Bible, and all sacred texts, are true and valuable when we
interpret them with humility, in Spirit and with Spirit.

True wisdom and awareness come from revelatory
experiences that words can trigger but cannot contain, and yet,
the words themselves are important. Readers cannot help but
bring their own mindsets and personal lenses to sacred texts,
and it is helpful to understand what they are, and experiment
with other lenses as well. Elias Hicks pointed out the danger
and potential hypocrisy of reading with one lens in his sermon
to Darby Meeting in 1826.

Now this seems to be so explained in the writings called
the Scriptures, that we might gain a great deal of profitable

instruction, if we would read them under the regulating influence of the spirit of God. But they can afford no instruction to those who read them in their own ability; for, if they depend on their own interpretation, they are as a dead letter, in so much, that those who profess to consider them the proper rule of faith and practice, will kill one another for the Scriptures' sake.[2]

One way to read humbly from within, with others, and with Spirit, is the Friendly Study Method (FSM) devised by Joanne Spears and Larry Spears. The Spears wanted to find a way to engage with the sacred texts like the Bible to feed on the same Life as George Fox, Margaret Fell, and others did. The Spears note that many "people remember Bible studies as occasions which encouraged sermonizing and authoritarian statements and discouraged questions. For these people, time spent in Bible study is remembered as fruitless for their spiritual lives and frustrating to the integrity of their own search for truth.... For many, the struggle to find or retain the core of faith, separate from childhood distortions and disappointments, is intense. It is for those people who have been away from Bible Study and who sense a need to turn in its direction that the following method for a Friendly Bible study is shared."[3]

Friendly Bible Study Questions (slightly revised)

1. What is the main point in this text? What are the words literally trying to convey? What is my lens in looking at the text? What are my assumptions?
2. What new light do I find in this particular reading of this passage of the text?

3. Is this passage true to my experience and my sense of identity or does it challenge the lens I am accustomed to? What happens if I see it with another lens?
4. What are the implications of this passage for my life?
5. What problems do I have with this passage? Is there a way for me to get past these problems?

The Spears offered a Quaker way into the Bible, a way formed from the central experience of the Light in our private lives, the reality of continuing revelation, and the connections between biblical witness and our present world. There are no leaders, there are only equal participants in reading, understanding, and discussing a passage. FSM offers these questions to clarify meanings, inspire new ways of thinking, and explore difficulties. My recent experience with David Curtis in his Woodbrooke course on the Gospel of Mary Magdalene was a good example of FSM. In that course, participants read various translations of a passage, pondered the prompts, and wrote for a while. Finally, participants each shared their answers in small groups and discussed the passage together as a whole group. Figure 4 is what one fellow participant, Margaret Kelso, wrote.

Because it is based on individual interpretation, sharing, and discussing with others in a safe and brave format, FSM accommodates Christian, theistic, and nontheistic theologies. It welcomes different spiritual languages and exploration of many social, ethnic, cultural, and religious lenses. With a few modifications, it can problematize normative ideas of race, supremacy, social class, sexuality, and gender identity. Friends could try on, as far as is possible, new points of view and new ideas, and discard old ways of thinking.

The Gospel of Mary

"Attachment to matter gives rise to incomparable suffering
because it goes against your true nature."

1. What is the main point in this text? What are the words literally trying to convey?

-----*Nothing will last as we conceive of it.*

2. What new light do I find in this reading of this passage of the text?

-----*An emphasis on interdependence - - What if Christianity had stressed this from the beginning?*

3. Is this passage true to my experience?

----- *Our connection to God is not a single or even multiple things, ideas, powers, recognitions, but the mesh of all creation.*

4. What are the implications of this passage for my life?

----- *Therefore, we need to respect and revere the unity of all things. I need to examine my life to see what I am clinging to.*

5. What problems do I have with this passage?

- - - - - *Living this truth within a world attached to 'attachment' is difficult.*
  I get a real sense of Maya (the illusion that this world is real).
  How does all this keep Spirit in my heart, keep me acting out of love?
  How does this move from my head to my heart?

Let's imagine switching lenses, like an eye doctor flips through different lenses to test our vision and fit glasses for our eyes. The new lenses are feminism, womanism, Black theology, and Queer theology. For instance, in an early feminist article, Phyllis Trible wrote that authorities use sacred texts as propaganda to support the unequal sociocultural positions of the sexes down through the ages.

> Born and bred in a land of patriarchy, the Bible abounds in male imagery and language. For centuries interpreters have explored and exploited this male language to articulate theology; to shape the contours and content of the church, synagogue and academy; and to instruct human beings — female and male — in who they are, what roles they should play, and how they should behave. So harmonious has seemed this association of Scripture with sexism, of faith with culture, that only a few have even questioned it.[4]

Trible identified three different approaches to evaluating the Bible. The first is a documentary lens on what a passage says or implies about the inferiority, subordination, and abuse of women, such as the story of Abraham's relationship to his wife, Sarah, and his concubine, Hagar. The second is a critical lens that seeks to change patriarchal assumptions by recovering, retranslating, and highlighting passages and stories that portray the divine as feminine, such as Proverbs 8 about Sophia/Chochma/Wisdom. The third lens is from the perspective of sisterhood, in which women's stories of survival are retold more sympathetically, making the women more active participants in the story. For instance, Jesus had six siblings, according to Mark 6, four brothers named James, Joseph, Judas and Simon, and two unnamed sisters. The sisterhood lens would ask why Mark did not know or report the sisters' names and what the sisters' lives might have been like.

However, women of color criticized the feminist approach as too narrowly focused on white women's issues. The womanist approach comes from the African American preaching tradition; it brings women's stories to the forefront, especially nameless servants or enslaved women. For instance, Wilda Gafney[5] discussed biblical women in terms of the factors that give them prestige/power or insignificance/peril. Analyzing factors like social class, sexuality, wealth, beauty, marriage, and fertility sheds new light on Bible stories. In Hebrew patriarch Abraham's complicated love life, his wife, Sarah, had high social class, property, and marriage, and yet she was infertile. The concubine, Hagar, was a slave; Sarah gave her to Abraham for his use because of her fertility, so Abraham could have a son. Hagar disdained the barren Sarah, and when Sarah later had her own baby, she drove Hagar and her son to a sure and painful death in the wilderness. Nevertheless, Hagar survived, and thus her story offers Black women a spirituality of survival. Delores Williams wrote,

My womanist reading of [the story of Hagar] sees God as responding to the African slave Hagar and her child in terms of survival strategies.... God's promise to Hagar throughout her story is one of survival (of her progeny) and not liberation. When they and their families get into serious social and economic straits, Black Christian women have believed that God helps them make a way out of no way.[6]

The womanist approach is a response to feminism but also to Black Liberation theology, which came out of the civil rights and Black Power movements in the United States in the mid-twentieth century. James H. Cone, author of many books about the Black spiritual experience, initiated Black Liberation theology. In his memoir, *Said I Wasn't Gonna Tell Nobody: The Making of a Black Theologian,* Cone described his disenchantment with white European theologians and theologies as he watched the rise of the Black Power movement in the cities around him. Cone took inspiration from the Black church community, the lives of writers like gay Black activist James Baldwin, and the spiritual songs and music expressing Black experience in a deeply racist country. His motivation to develop a Black theology was his profound frustration with the centuries of struggle to achieve civil rights in the United States.

Cone thought that white Christian theology at its best did not help Black people achieve equality and dignity, and at its worst, it intentionally kept Black people in positions of inferiority and subservience. He reconceived biblical symbols to give meaning to their suffering and death. Most telling was the analogy between the cruel wooden cross that killed Jesus and the brutal lynching trees of the United States, where innocent people of color were/are unjustly tortured and murdered. To be honest, I could barely listen to his book *The Cross and the Lynching Tree;*

it was a painful lens for me to try to assume, and yet it changed me more than many theoretical discussions about anti-racism.

Cone saw that white Christians and their churches were foundational in a structure of institutional racism, when the Gospel, had they read it and understood it properly, should have made them brothers and sisters to the poor and oppressed. Inspired by the many Bible stories that raised up liberation as a goal, he wrote, "By electing Israelite slaves as the people of God and by becoming the Oppressed One in Jesus Christ, the human race is made to understand that God is known where human beings experience humiliation and suffering.... Liberation is not an afterthought, but the very essence of divine activity."[7]

"Queering" the Bible means looking at the passages with transgressive lenses and with resistance to the power and authority of the "normal," sometimes by adding contextual information and sometimes by reinterpreting. For instance, Nehemiah, the effective and compassionate leader of the Hebrew community after their return from captivity, may have been a eunuch, a male servant castrated to guarantee his loyalty to his sovereign, Cyrus. Thus, besides a compassionate leader, he was a social outsider or outcast, and we must read his plaintive prayers like this in 5 Nehemiah 19: "Remember me with favor, my God, for all I have done for these people" in light of his ambiguous status and sacrifice.[8]

Certain Bible passages have been used against people who identify as LGBTQ, so it is highly appropriate to problematize gendered assumptions and heterosexual expectations. "Clobber texts" like Genesis 1–2 and 19:1–38, Leviticus 18:22 and 20:13, Romans 1:25–27 and others are cited to argue that heterosexuality is the only natural way to be in the Judeo-Christian world. Theologian Amy-Jill Levine suggests starting with humility. "We do not know and cannot know what was in the mind of the authors and redactors of Genesis or Leviticus or the relevant

New Testament passages; we do not know and cannot know what the first people to receive these works thought. In many of the clobber passages, we do not even know, for certain, to what the text refers."[9] In 1 Genesis 28, the Divine commands humans to be fruitful and multiply, which for some people means that they should engage in sexual intercourse for procreation only if they are fertile and married. However, Levine points out that the text is never a specific limitation of sexual union or pleasure, just a command to fill the earth with people.

Queering Sophia/Chochma/Wisdom from 8 Proverbs in the Hebrew Bible means looking at her brash immodesty as subversive and calling her "wisdom in drag." What does the phrase "in drag" say about Wisdom's fearless embodiment as a human? How does Wisdom let her life speak? Elizabeth Stuart wrote that "so excessive is her performance that previous understandings of [W]isdom are blown apart. She is the prudent, excellent and wise wife whose virtues are extolled in Proverbs played to excess, taken from the closeted environments of the family and into the street. She performs her outrageously enlarged character on the street corners and at the city gates, the busiest places in town."[10]

To me, these different lenses evoke the kind of reading that theologian Barbara Holmes calls *griosh*, a fusion of Bible study and lectio divina. *Griosh* derives from *griot*, a word for African storytellers, historians, and keepers of cultural memory. She felt that the sound *sh* was a marker of the *hush arbors* or *brush arbors*, the secret places where enslaved individuals practiced their spiritual traditions in private, where they developed their own Black perspectives on Christianity. *Griosh* is a participatory communal dialogue that combines religious memory, contextual interpretation, and imaginative juxtapositions. In the practice of *griosh*, readers read liberation and empowerment for everyone into the texts. "Like lectio divina, *griosh* is a contemplative reading of Holy Scripture, a method of interpreting the incomprehensible situation of slavery."[11] Griosh is another way to read and understand sacred texts with Spirit Within.

Any kind of open-minded and transgressive, imaginative, Spirit-led Bible study might encourage Friends to find inspiration and guidance for others and ourselves through encounters in which we become aware of our prejudices and implicit beliefs. Joan Chittister thought that we should "grapple with a holy idea until its depth and call reshape our souls. To get it, as the Chinese proverb says, a drop at a time until it wears away our hard-heartedness like water dripping on a rock. Then, when we have scraped off the outer layer of an old and, we thought, hackneyed idea, we see it afresh and it shows us the way to a new dimension of spiritual life."[12] If Friends see the world afresh, the new vision might generate, besides personal revelation, vocal ministry to others who, like me, long to hear others' encounters with holy and subversive ideas in worship.

Endnotes

1   Merton, Thomas, "Lectio Divina," *Cistercian Studies Quarterly* 50.1 2015, p. 5–37

2   Hicks, Elias, "The Blood of Jesus: A Sermon and Prayer at Darby Meeting," Philadelphia Yearly Meeting, 1826. *The Quaker*, Vol. I No. 1 Undated, pp. 1–22.

3   Spears, Joanne and Larry Spears. Retrieved 1/2/2023 from http://www.read-the-bible.org/friendlybiblestudy.htm

4   Trible, Phyllis, "Feminist Hermeneutics and Biblical Studies," *Christian Century*, 1982. Retrieved 8/14/2023 from https://www.religion-online.org/article/feminist-hermeneutics-and-biblical-studies/

5   Gafney, Wilda, *Womanist Midrash: A Reintroduction to the Women of the Torah and the Throne*, John Knox Press, 2017. Kindle edition.

6   Delores Williams, *Sisters in the Wilderness*, Orbis Books, 1993, p. 196.

7   Cone, James, *A Black Theology of Liberation* (40th anniversary Ed.). Orbis Books 2010, p. 67.

8   Stanley, Ron. L, "Ezra-Nehemiah," in *The Queer Bible Commentary* Ed. by Deryn Guest, Robert E. Goss, Mona West, and Thomas Bohache, SCM Press, 2015, p. 271.

9   Levine, Amy-Jill, "Clobber Passages," Retrieved 6/3/2023 from https://outreach.faith/2022/09/amy-jill-levine-how-to-read-the-bibles-clobber-passages-on-homosexuality/

10   Stuart, Elizabeth. "Proverbs," *The Queer Bible Commentary* Ed. by Deryn Guest, Robert E. Goss, Mona West, and Thomas Bohache, SCM Press, 2015, p. 328.

11   Holmes, Barbara, *Joy Unspeakable: Contemplative Practices of the Black Church*, Fortress Press, 2004, p. 120.

12   Chittister, Joan, *The Monastic Heart: 50 Simple Practices for a Contemplative and Fulfilling Life*, Convergent Books, 2021, p 193.

Chapter 10

Practicing Lectio Divina

"Alas, Lord," I said, "I do not know how to speak; I
am too young."
But the Lord said to me, "Do not say, 'I am too young.'
You must go to everyone I send you to and say
whatever I command you.
Do not be afraid of them, for I am with you and will
rescue you," declares the Lord.
Then the Lord reached out his hand and touched my
mouth
and said to me, "I have put my words in your mouth.
See, today I appoint you over nations and kingdoms
to uproot and tear down,
to destroy and overthrow, to build and to plant."

1 Jeremiah 6–10

The prophet Jeremiah made excuses for his reluctance to offer
vocal ministry. He did not know how to speak; he was too
young, too humble, and too inexperienced to have anything
to say. However, the Divine called him to speak his truth and
vowed to rescue him if he needed it. In a poignant moment,
Spirit reached out to Jeremiah, touched his mouth, and put
the right words in his mouth. He called him to be fearless in
prophecy. Later, in 15 Jeremiah 16, Jeremiah declared, "When
your words came, I ate them; they were my joy and my heart's
delight, for I bear your name, Lord God Almighty [e.g., I am
yours; I carry your name to others.]."

I have been telling the story of *lectio divina* as the story of
how the Divine puts the Word into human mouths, providing
sacred words, and demanding that we eat them so we can speak

in prophetic voices for our time. Down through the millennia, revelation and prophecy are the powers associated with lectio divina.

Prophecy might start with reading and studying sacred texts, agreeing and disagreeing with them, and problematizing the words and ideas, but we cannot limit ourselves to intellectual discussions if we want to understand from within. Father Romano Guardini recognized that the Word penetrates our hearts and souls deeply.

> The divine word must be considered as whole words, with shape and sound. To focus our attention only on the intelligible concept expressed by them would be folly. It would be rootless intellectual theory. A word is a wondrous reality: form and content, significance and love, intellect and heart, a full, round, vibrant whole. It is not barren information for us to consider and understand but a reality for us to encounter personally. We must receive it and store it in all its earthiness, its characteristic style and imagery. Then it proves its power.[1]

Lectio divina challenges the status quo, and yet, it works best if the passage resonates without a lot of cognitive dissonance. Pray-ers must overlook any resistances so the deep metaphors and images germinate in the soul, or they are better off choosing a different passage to speak to their soul without resistance. The soul is where the mind responds to the wonder of the Word and the heart hears the power the Word evokes. Lectio ultimately leads into contemplation, that is, into prayer, union with the Divine, transformation, and a different way of living in the world. Catholic theologian James Finley wrote, "Lectio Divina is a grace state of consciousness that we can actively choose to cultivate that puts us into intimate awareness of God's presence in our life."[2]

As a devotional preparation, lectio divina encourages ministry that leads to a deepened silence in waiting worship. Rufus Jones wrote that vocal ministry in Meeting for Worship is a living thing that grows. He wrote,

> There is a place, an important place, for brief testimony, for the few words of experience, or of Scripture reference, or of quotation from the ripe experience of others, but there ought to be much oftener than usually happens that other type of ministry which opens windows for the soul, and which raises the whole level of life for the entire congregation. Such a message ought to be followed by a deepened silence, and if more words are said after the silence, they should, if possible, fit and carry on the message that has spread over the meeting. Preaching, if it is true preaching, ought not to interrupt the worship; it ought to continue the spirit of worship.[3]

There are many good ways to practice lectio divina and no way is wrong if it helps Friends make the words of a sacred passage their own. This is a way to practice Quaker testimonies of ecospirituality, peace, equality, and social justice through continuing revelation and prophecy. It leaves a holy space for all Friends to enter.

Lectio divina: Reading with the Indwelling

Ground the practice in earth-loving spirituality, in union with *being*.

Hear, read, and understand a sacred passage filtered through Spirit.

> Welcome different metaphors, myths, lenses and languages with open receptivity.
>
> Embrace imagination, visualization, play, ritual, and art to interpret the sacred words.
>
> Look into, under, and beyond the words to understand the Word.
>
> Absorb the Word into the body: the brain, heart, muscles, and gut.
>
> Ruminate on the Word in a continual attunement with Spirit.
>
> Follow the Divine into revelation, contemplation and silence.
>
> Nurture the potential for prophetic ministry.

Lectio divina seems simple at the beginning. The formulation of the method is credited to a Carthusian monk named Guigo II who lived in France in the twelfth century. Guigo II wrote a book called *The Ladder of Monks*, making an analogy to Jacob's dream in 12 Genesis 12 in which angels ascended a staircase to God carrying prayers up and descended with divine answers. He laid out four steps of ascending awareness of the Divine: *lectio* (reading), *meditatio* (thinking about), *oratio* (praying), and *contemplatio* (internal stillness and awareness of the presence of God). We start in silence, understanding that we ground ourselves on the earth and in *being*, and we remember all of the humans before us who yearned to open to Spirit. We humbly ask Spirit to enter us and be with us in the room. At any point in the process, we return to silence, or we take time for writing. This process can be adapted as a solitary discipline.

1. **Lectio**: When led out of the silence by Spirit, one person reads the passage aloud while others listen. Several others read it aloud too, while everyone follows along.

We look at the words and phrases, considering what positive or negative emotions or memories they bring to us. We study the text with an open mind using the Friendly Study Method (or similar), discussing the main point(s), the lens(es) we are reading with, and exploring the truthfulness according to our experience. We mention any problems or obstacles we might have with the text because of our memories or associations, trying to overcome these. We try to consider the text through another lens, one that might be a stretch for us.

2. **Meditatio**: We use the other steps from the Friendly Study Method during this phase. What new light does the text hold for us/me, in light of the lens we/I usually use? What implications does the text have for our lives, understanding, spirituality and future? In silence, we ponder the meaning of the text in a personal way. We might take the time to write some notes in a journal, in *scriptio divina*.

3. **Oratio**: We enter more deeply into silence, letting words go, and centering in wordless prayer and waiting worship. We open ourselves to the Divine, and to any wisdom and love we might receive in the form of vocal ministry. If in a group, we speak the vocal ministry. If alone, we write the ministry.

4. **Contemplatio**: If way opens, we let go of all thought and sink into a deep rest in the Divine Presence in our lives. "Contemplation is different. In contemplation we wrestle with the meaning behind all those words and phrases. We begin to realize the presence of God in life. In our own lives. We become more concentrated on knowing the mind of God rather than limiting the spiritual life to the traditional use of religious things—candles and incense, chant and prayer forms—as magnetic and enriching as they are.... Contemplation is not a spiritual 'practice' in

the normal sense of the word. It is the end-product of all those spiritual practices that have led you to the heart of God and the awareness of God in your heart, in your mind, in your life choices, wrapped round in an aura of God-consciousness that is beyond any need for words or for spiritual exercises."[4]

5. **Scriptio:** Scriptio divina is a way of reverently copying, dictating, and writing sacred passages, by hand if possible, into a journal. The experiences that we have while reading prayerfully form the basis for further devotional reflection in writing. For Presbyterian minister Eugene Peterson sacred reading and writing are both ways of conversing while in mysterious and holy relationship with the Divine. "What I mean to insist upon is that spiritual writing—Spirit-sourced writing—requires spiritual reading, a reading that honors words as holy, words as basic means of forming an intricate web of relationships between God and the human, between all things visible and invisible."[5] In meditatio, we might write our questions and answers, in oratio, we might write our prayers, in contemplatio, we might write about what we experience.

6. **Ora et Labora (Walking Meditation):** For a long time, I was quite content with practicing this five-part sequence alone or occasionally with a small group of Friends. Then I read about how early prophets ate the scrolls, that is, they learned the sacred words by heart, and how monks and nuns ruminated on sacred passages and mumbled them as a constant attunement with the Divine as they went about their day in *ora et labora* (pray and work). I learned that early Friends who were mighty preachers and writers memorized biblical passes so that they were handy in ministry and writing. Looking back and reflecting on my

practice, I see that during the weeks and months that we were in lockdown together, sacred reading and writing evolved into a walking prayer. While I ambled aimlessly around my neighborhood reconstructing the meaning of the passages in my head, I matched my steps to the words I recollected.

Recently, I made the Camino de Santiago, a pilgrimage path in Spain, where I consciously practiced walking meditation by memorizing and ruminating on favorite Quaker quotes like James Nayler's reference to 3 Revelation 20, where the Christ says, "Here I am! I stand at the door and knock. If anyone hears my voice and opens the door, I will come in and eat with them, and they with me." Nayler's understanding was more about filling ourselves with the Light of Christ

by supping continually with him, and he with you, will you come so to be filled with him, that all haste and impatience and distrust will be covered and overcome with him, and so your mortal be swallowed up of the immortal, till it become your whole life and being; and all your thoughts, words and actions have their rise and being therein; so that self be seen no more.[6]

Another favorite passage is Isaac Penington's definition of Love.

What is love? What shall I say of it, or how shall I in words express its nature? It is the sweetness of life; it is the sweet, tender, melting nature of God, flowing up through his seed of life into the creature, and of all things making the creature most like unto himself, both in nature and operation. It fulfils the law, it fulfils the gospel; it wraps up all in one, and brings forth all in the oneness. It excludes all evil out of the heart, it perfects all good in the heart. A touch of love doth this in measure; perfect love doth this in fullness.[7]

Before I left on the pilgrimage, I wrote the quotes by hand on small notecards so that I could look at them while walking with my friends and fellow pilgrims. I emulated Benedictine monks and nuns for whom lectio divina was an all-day activity. As I walked the Camino, I thought up hand/arm gestures to embody the words in the quote and assist in recall; and practiced them under my rain poncho.

Memorization and repetition became body prayer and walking meditation when my own narrative thought gave way to rumination on the quotes. When I tired of this and needed a boost, when it was raining hard, and my poncho and cowl enveloped my body, I listened to Paulette Meier's Quaker plainsong chants[8] on an old mp3 player. It was magical, mystical, and monkish. I was on a spiritual pilgrimage, and I meant to walk with the Indwelling Spirit. The practice helped me internalize the Word in my heart, soul, mind, and body. I began to feel accompanied by Spirit in a way reminiscent of Brother Lawrence: "I make it my business only to persevere in his holy presence, wherein I keep myself by a simple attention, and a general fond regard to God, which I may call an actual presence of God ... an habitual silent, and secret conversation of the soul with God."[9]

However, when I reconsidered Brother Lawrence's way of practicing the presence, I understood that there were some distinctions in my practice of walking meditation. Brother Lawrence's God was a transcendent and interventionist man-God and his conversations with God were *I/Thou*. "My God, I am wholly thine. O God of Love, I love thee with all my heart...." (p. 80). At present, I am not able to have an *I/thou* conversation with the Divine because it is dualistic. To me, the Divine is a cosmic and incarnate noninterventionist force of *being*, Presence, Satyagraha, Love, or Oneness, and I intentionally keep nonduality out of *being*. I do not use pronouns, so I am not able to address the Indwelling Divine as a *thou*. My sense of attunement is a different kind of conversation in relationship to the Divine Within.

I don't want to overstate things. I don't see angels or hear heavenly trumpets. I still have my ups and downs. Quotes and verses in my heart memory are mantras as I walk or do household tasks. Repetition is a comforting and soothing soundtrack while going through my day, but I do not always need to use words, and the feeling stays as an undercurrent to my existence, attuning me to the Divine. My sense of isolation and duality disappeared, and the insidious left-brained idea that the Divine is out there in the distance, disinterested in me, or judging me vanished. I no longer hear the voice of the inner critic as loudly because Love drowns it out. Gratitude and praise are in my heart and in my body, as a background to my life. It is worship.

Did sacred reading and writing transform my experience in Meeting? Yes, in small but, I believe, important ways. The long, dry season of empty silence has loosened its grip on me. An expansive *being* during Meeting gathers all Friends in worship, and I am part of it. During worship, I feel the Presence, the awareness of Spirit that takes me from analytical thought to heart prayer to steady attunement for a time. I feel stirrings to share my growing understandings in ministry more confidently, in a way that, I hope, contributes to the worship. I always hunger for holy and subversive ministry from other Friends. Thomas Kelly wrote,

> Begin now, as you read these words, as you sit in your chair, to offer your whole selves, utterly and in joyful abandon, in quiet, glad surrender to [the Presence]

Within. In secret ejaculations of praise, turn in humble wonder to the Light, faint though it may be. Keep contact with the outer world of sense and meanings. Here is no discipline in absent-mindedness. Walk and talk and work and laugh with your friends. But behind the scenes, keep up the life of simple prayer and inward worship.[10]

Endnotes

1   Guardini, Romano, *Meditations before Mass*, Sophia Institute Press, 1993, p. 66.

2   Finley, James, "Turning to Guigo II with James Finley," Retrieved 7/5/2022 from the Center for Action and Contemplation. //efaidnbmnnnibpcajpcglclefindmkaj/ https://cac.org/wp-content/uploads/2021/10/TTTM_Transcript_TTGLM.pdf

3   Jones, Rufus, "The Vital Cell," Retrieved 8/8/2020 from https://quaker.org/legacy/pamphlets/wpl1941a.html

4   Chittister, Joan. *The Monastic Heart: 50 Simple Practices for a Contemplative and Fulfilling Life*, Convergent Books, 2021, pp. 193–6.

5   Peterson, Eugene, *Eat this Book: A Conversation in the Art of Spiritual Reading*, William Erdmans, 2006. Chapter 1, Kindle Edition.

6   Nayler, James, *Milk for Babes and Meat for Strong Men A Feast of Fat Things* printed for Robert Wilson, at the sign of the Black-Spread-Eagle and Wind-Mill in Martins le Grand, London, 1661.

7   Penington, Isaac, Retrieved from *Faith and Practice* of the British Yearly Meeting https://qfp.quaker.org.uk/passage/26-30/.

8   Meier, Paulette, https://www.paulettemeier.com/timeless-quaker-wisdom-in-plainsong.html

9   Brother Lawrence, *The Practice of the Presence of God,* Grand Rapids, MI: Spire 1967. p. 36

10 Kelly, Thomas, "The Light Within" in *A Testament of Devotion* Harper Collins Publishing, 1941, pp. 38–39.

About the Author

Barbara Birch is a white cisgendered middle class woman baby boomer trained as an academic in the field of applied linguistics. She tells stories by collecting and connecting quotes. This is the story of how she sees lectio divina as a Quaker practice. Raised in a mainstream Christian denomination, she fell away from the church and Christianity as a teen, when she could no longer believe in a punitive god who sacrificed his son's life to redeem her from teenage sin so that she could go to heaven after death. She could not believe in a deity who wanted uncritical adoration from people kneeling, standing, sitting and singing in unison, or whose earthly leaders refused to allow her to minister because of her gender. She believed that these indictments meant that there was no God and all religion was bogus, because she did not know any other way to worship and could not conceive of any other kind of God.

After drifting around the world for a couple of decades, she was an angry 30-something single mother graduate student badly in need of a community for spiritual support. She found the local Friends Meeting in Madison, WI, and felt at home in the silent worship immediately. As she sat in the silence week after week, her anger slipped off her, and she learned to listen to the still small voice inside. She started to think that Spirit guided her and she became a member of the Meeting. Now in her seventies, she lives in the Bay Area with her family and belongs to Strawberry Creek Meeting in Berkeley, CA.

Note to the Reader

Dear Reader,

Thank you for purchasing *Lectio Divina: Revelation and Prophecy*. I hope you got as much out of reading this book as I did writing it. If you enjoyed the book and have a comment, please add a review of the book to your favorite online site. If you would like to connect with me, I am on Facebook at facebook.com/birch. barbara. You can also follow me on Medium. I would love to hear from you.

Yours in Peace,
Barbara Birch

THE NEW OPEN SPACES

Throughout the two thousand years of Christian tradition
there have been, and still are, groups and individuals
that exist in the margins and upon the edge of faith. But
in Christianity's contrapuntal history it has often been
these outcasts and pioneers that have forged contemporary
orthodoxy out of former radicalism as belief evolves to engage
with and encompass the ever-changing social and scientific
realities. Real faith lies not in the comfortable certainties of
the Orthodox, but somewhere in a half-glimpsed hinterland
on the dirt track to Emmaus, where the Death of God meets
the Resurrection, where the supernatural Christ meets the
historical Jesus, and where the revolution liberates
both the oppressed and the oppressors.

Welcome to Christian Alternative... a space at the
edge where the light shines through.
If you have enjoyed this book, why not tell other readers
by posting a review on your preferred book site.

Recent bestsellers from Christian Alternative are:

Bread Not Stones
The Autobiography of An Eventful Life
Una Kroll
The spiritual autobiography of a truly remarkable
woman and a history of the struggle for ordination in the
Church of England.
Paperback: 978-1-78279-804-0 ebook: 978-1-78279-805-7

The Quaker Way
A Rediscovery
Rex Ambler
Although fairly well known, Quakerism is not well
understood. The purpose of this book is to explain how
Quakerism works as a spiritual practice.
Paperback: 978-1-78099-657-8 ebook: 978-1-78099-658-5

Blue Sky God
The Evolution of Science and Christianity
Don MacGregor
Quantum consciousness, morphic fields and blue-sky
thinking about God and Jesus the Christ.
Paperback: 978-1-84694-937-1 ebook: 978-1-84694-938-8

Celtic Wheel of the Year
Tess Ward
An original and inspiring selection of prayers combining
Christian and Celtic Pagan traditions, and interweaving
their calendars into a single pattern of prayer for
every morning and night of the year.
Paperback: 978-1-90504-795-6

Christian Atheist

Belonging without Believing

Brian Mountford

Christian Atheists don't believe in God but miss him:
especially the transcendent beauty of his music,
language, ethics, and community.

Paperback: 978-1-84694-439-0 ebook: 978-1-84694-929-6

Compassion Or Apocalypse?

A Comprehensible Guide to the Thoughts of René Girard

James Warren

How René Girard changes the way we think about
God and the Bible, and its relevance for our
apocalypse-threatened world.

Paperback: 978-1-78279-073-0 ebook: 978-1-78279-072-3

Diary Of A Gay Priest

The Tightrope Walker

Rev. Dr. Malcolm Johnson

Full of anecdotes and amusing stories, but the Church
is still a dangerous place for a gay priest.

Paperback: 978-1-78279-002-0 ebook: 978-1-78099-999-9

Readers of ebooks can buy or view any of these bestsellers by
clicking on the live link in the title. Most titles are published in
paperback and as an ebook. Paperbacks are available
in traditional bookshops. Both print and ebook
formats are available online.

Find more titles and sign up to our readers' newsletter at
www.collectiveinkbooks.com/christianity Follow us on
Facebook at https://www.facebook.com/ChristianAlternative

Also in this series

Quaker Quicks - Practical Mystics
Quaker Faith in Action
Jennifer Kavanagh
ISBN: 978-1-78904-279-5

Quaker Quicks - Hearing the Light
The core of Quaker theology
Rhiannon Grant
ISBN: 978-1-78904-504-8

Quaker Quicks - In STEP with Quaker Testimony
Simplicity, Truth, Equality and Peace - inspired by
Margaret Fell's writings
Joanna Godfrey Wood
ISBN: 978-1-78904-577-2

Quaker Quicks - Telling the Truth About Go
Quaker approaches to theology
Rhiannon Grant
ISBN: 978-1-78904-081-4

Quaker Quicks - Money and Soul
Quaker Faith and Practice and the Economy
Pamela Haines
ISBN: 978-1-78904-089-0

Quaker Quicks - Hope and Witness in Dangerous Times
Lessons from the Quakers On Blending Faith, Daily Life, and Activism
J. Brent Bill
ISBN: 978-1-78904-619-9

Quaker Quicks - In Search of Stillness
Using a simple meditation to find inner peace
Joanna Godfrey Wood
ISBN: 978-1-78904-707-3